TEES

The Art of the T-Shirt

by MAKI

CONTENTS

PREFACE

I was about sixteen years old when I designed my first T-shirt. My football team was going to play in an international tournament in Germany and we wanted something special for that. I tried to create the best shirt ever. I was so proud when the printed shirts arrived and even more so when the whole team was wearing them. Looking back at the design now, it's by far the worst T-shirt design I've ever done. Using several free fonts in combination with a few clip-art illustrations seemed like such a good idea back then ... Still, the feeling of having my design printed and worn by my friends was great. Now, almost 12 years later, I still get excited when a new T-shirt design arrives from the printers.

In a way, T-shirt design started our international career – not at the football tournament in Germany, but at an online T-shirt design competition called Threadless. Winning that contest brought new people to our website, which made us switch it from Dutch to English. Eventually this led to several new jobs, many of them T-shirt designs. We've done hundreds now.

Making all these tees strongly influenced our style. We were forced to work with a limited colour palette. Working with fewer colours has not only made our work better, it has almost become a trademark in all of our creations.

Therefore, designing T-shirts can have an impact on the way you work as an artist. It can even influence your personal life. Marc Hendrick of Das Monk met his girlfriend when she came over to him to tell him how much she liked his shirt, which he had designed himself. T-shirts may well be the next big thing in bringing two people together. It might be a good idea to start a dating agency that prints specially designed tees for singles. "I have been alone for 23 years, but I do have hobbies" might be a good line for someone who is desperate.

New T-shirt stores pop up daily on the Internet. It seems impossible that all these different stores can survive and, indeed, it is. Many stores bomb within a year. Still, it's an exciting territory. There are online shops for everyone – for the computer nerd, the arty type and the tasteless. The great thing is that you can buy your piece of apparel from the other side of the world and be pretty sure that none of your friends will have the same thing. Internet stores have the flexibility to create new shirts every day and sell them online immediately, while regular shops usually depend on their seasonal collections. Larger chains don't have much flexibility. For marketing reasons, they have to know what their collections will look like one year before they come out. The big disadvantage with online shops is that you can't try the shirt on before purchasing it.

THE BOOK

As the title implies, this is a book about T-shirts. It's a showcase of contemporary T-shirt designs ranged by designer. Besides showing the artwork, the book unveils something about the person behind it. How do they work? Why are T-shirts such an interesting medium to work on? Would they wear their own shirts?

Every graphic designer or illustrator designs a tee at a certain point in life, whether it's for a friend's birthday party or a well-paid job for a huge denim brand. We've collected the work of more than 80 artists from around the world. You'll find a large diversity of styles, techniques and flavours, from well-known designers as well as "fresh meat". This selection will give a good impression of what's happening in T-shirt design these days. The variety shows that almost anything goes, though there are a few trends. Big prints are popular. There's also an increasing number of designers who try to make the world a better place by making environmentally friendly T-shirts. They don't do this by having a slogan like "Green Tees" or "Don't Kill Cute Bunnies" on the chest, but by using environmentally sound materials.

Although this book isn't supposed to be a catalogue, we have included websites where the shirts are (or were) for sale on the contact pages at the end of the book. Not all tees have been designed to sell, but for personal promotion, limited editions or other projects. If you want to find out more about a shirt, you can always check out the designer's website.

Enjoy!

Matthijs Maat
MAKI

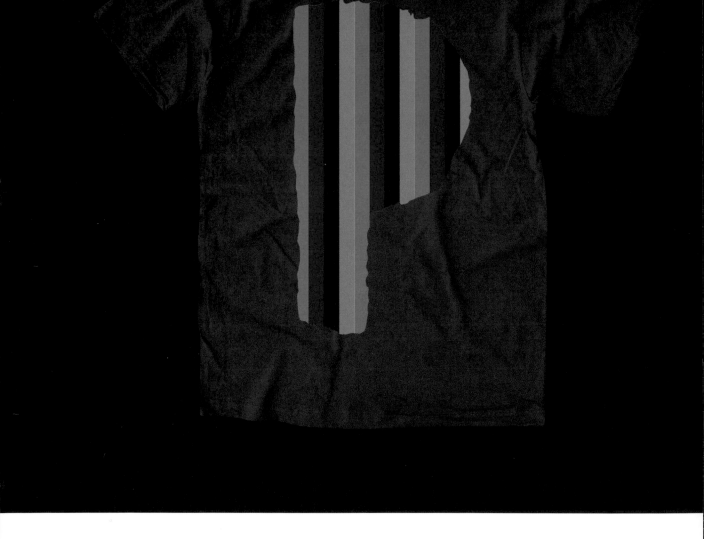

The Netherlands
www.pimpalicious.com

PIMPALICIOUS LIVING

I try to spread a positive message. I want everybody to get his or her life on point and live a Pimpalicious Lifestyle; that's a positive state of mind in which my team and I are already living. Hell yeah, I wear my own shirts! And if you could, you should! I am the core of this Pimpalicious Living state of mind; if I want other people to follow me and join me, I need to believe in myself first! All my designs are hand-drawn, and mostly typographic. I only use the computer to work the sketches.

I work in different ways and with different materials: pencils; markers; Indian ink and a small brush; ripped pieces of paper; and whatever makes that specific design look fresh and funky. When designing a shirt, I keep in mind that other people are going to wear this. I try to make it appealing.

Chopped & Chic

Step Your Game Up

Man Made Money Made Men

Funky Fresh In The Flesh

Flame Of The City

It's A Mad Mad World

Only One Can Win

P-Stripes

I Am Somebody

The Hottest Of The Hot

Top Of The Line

Turn Dreams Into Cash

Anything ...

Pointu

Desktop User

RAPHAËL GARNIER

There isn't any concept behind my T-shirt designs. For me a T-shirt is not conceptual, I just search for the beauty. It's a way of "giving life" to my graphics. These designs were created with serigraphy on a tee. The T-shirt is a norm, and it's interesting to play with a norm. I have never met anyone wearing one of my shirts. I'm afraid of this idea because I don't control people. If a man wears my tee with a very bad style ... my design becomes, for me, a bad design in my head. My inspiration is a list of great people: Peter Kogler, Maurice Sendak, Giordano Bruno, Serge Dano, Mathias Schweizer, Georges Méliès, Athanase Kirchner. T-shirt designing is FUN, although I do it only occasionally. The problem with T-shirt design is the time between your drawing and the date when your tee is in a shop. It's too long.

France
www.raphaelgarnier.com

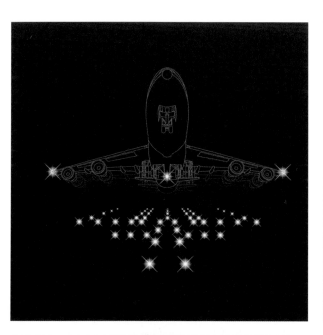

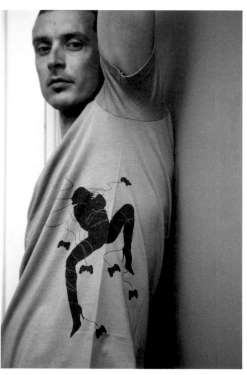

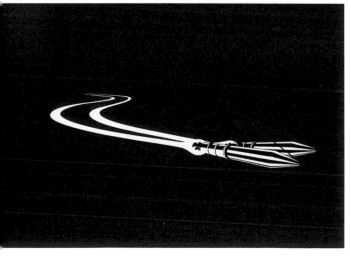

Take Off

Iniohos

Console

MANDOLINI

Online boutique Supermandolini was launched in 2007 by the graphic designers Emanuel Lakoutsis and Ellie Kakoulidou. The pair, who hail from Thessaloniki, Greece, have used their design skills and fashion savvy to create a well-rounded boutique, offering graphic tees for men and women, art-inspired home wares and a great variety of jewellery. They also control all aspects of the brand's visual presence, from the product designs themselves all the way to web design, packaging, photography and promotion. Makes you wonder how two people can manage to design and run a boutique of this level, but if you are passionate about what you do, then the sky is the limit.

Greece
www.supermandolini.com

Cupid Bazooka

Against The Odds

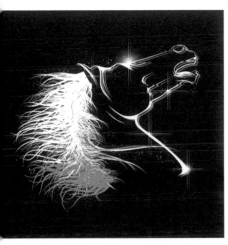

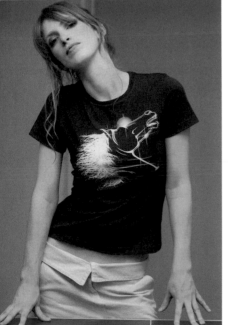

Stallion

Digital Punk

Germany
www.violent-elegance.com

VIOLENT ELEGANCE

In designing my T-shirts, I put an emphasis on "keeping it simple". Characteristic of my designs are simple shapes with high contrast, black and white, and acid colours. The materials I use are watercolours mixed with half-tone raster. My main inspiration is the forest. The advantage of designing T-shirts is seeing them all over the world. I make this possible by offering free shipping worldwide. I primarily do art direction for big international brands. Therefore, T-shirt designing is a great balance for me. And, yes, I wear my own T-shirts!

Triangle

Square

Circle

MATT PALMER

Australia
www.letsmakeart.com

My T-shirts are generally a distorted look at reality. I have quite a morbid sense of humour, so often my illustrations represent a fairly normal situation with a subtle but darkly humorous twist. I understand that technically I am not a fantastic illustrator. Concepts that suit, or even benefit from, a more haphazard approach will often become a priority among my many ideas. I love the printed page, but there is nothing like the challenge of designing something that will relate to its wearer and be proudly shown on their torso. It's great when other people enjoy my art, but it's not a great motivation of mine. Having worked as a commercial designer and in marketing for a long time, I understand that there is a fan base for everything. So long as I am happy with what I am making, I know others will be too.

Inside You

Lets Make Art.

Mein Bad!

Grow a Beard

They Are All Winners

Today's Top Story

KEVIN SCOTT HAILEY
COMA AND COTTON

USA
www.comaandcotton.com

White Black Bear

White Animal Kingdom

Coma and Cotton is a San Francisco-based company encompassing imagery and design by artist Kevin Scott Hailey. The artwork is inspired by his travels to South America, as well as Native American mythology and psychedelic experience. Coma and Cotton avoids many of the trappings of contemporary shirt labels by emphasizing abstraction over symbolism. By hand drawing each shirt, without referencing any sourced art, the imagery maintains its originality, even if the evoked sentimentality is familiar. Despite Hailey's insistence that fashion, particularly shirts, is disposable, he nonetheless must satisfy himself of each work's worth before allowing it to be sold. However, that disposability — the temporality of each shirt's lifespan — allows Hailey simultaneously to embrace and disown them, a practice he likens to a Tibetan mandala. Coma and Cotton shirts are now sold wholesale to boutiques across the United States, as well as online, at shows and to private parties.

Burnout Black Mushroom

Red Animal Kingdom

White Burnout Mandala

This Ain't No Half Steppin'

KAROLY
Hungary
www.extraverage.net
KIRALYFALVI

These T-shirts were realized in past years as personal projects in limited quantities for sale in Budapest and online. My logos or graphics are made to work on any surface; they are words/sentences/buzzwords to share the leading ideas in a bold way. My T-shirt designs are typographic and include letter-based graphics and clean vectors. For me, designing T-shirts is no different from making other designs. I do not see many limitations; I love to print shirts in any way, on any material and with any technique. It feels great if people love what I do, especially if they agree with the concept or message! Everyday life, people, artists and friends, in addition to electronic music, inspire me. Designing T-shirts enables me to spread the word, to let people see my world. I design T-shirts as a hobby I love, and sometimes for groups or companies.

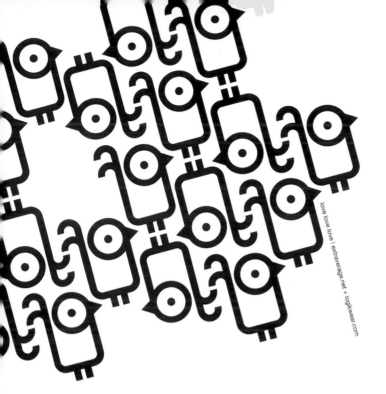

Logo Birds

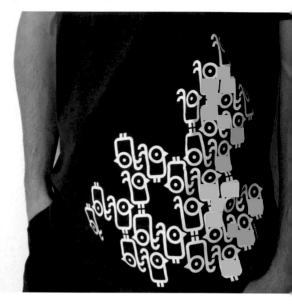

SUPERDOPE EXTRAVERAGE IS OVERDOING THE EXTREMES
LOGIKWEAR.COM BRINGS YOU THE BLING BLING

Super Top Notch DeLuxe

It varies from image to image, but generally I create elements by hand (using spray paint, Play-Doh, pens, etc.), and also by drawing in Illustrator, and then I combine these elements in Photoshop. However, this is not a strict rule by any means ... sometimes I will create an image entirely in Illustrator and other times almost all by hand. All the T-shirts I have ever designed have had a very open briefing with the client, I use them to try out ideas I have had for personal work. I don't wear my own work because I get bored with it after having spent however long staring at it while making it. There is also the problem that I always seem to be sent the wrong size by the clients so they never fit anyway! I'm currently designing T-shirts of my own; perhaps I will print one for myself that fits properly.

UK
wilson2000.com

STEVEN WILSON

Ribbon Tiger

Camo Faces

Man Smoking A Pipe

JEFF FINLEY

USA
www.gomedia.us

Jeff Finley is part-owner of Go Media and has been designing professionally for five years. In addition to designing tees, Jeff also does package design, logos, posters and runs a popular design blog at www.gomediazine.com. The concepts of his designs vary from shirt to shirt. Generally, he wants to make a bold visual statement in a creative way that makes people notice. From time to time, he wears his own shirts. Sometimes he's not interested in making a bold statement, so his tees aren't always what he's in the mood for when he gets up in the morning. His shirts are all created digitally and often with a Wacom tablet. The designs featured were all created in Photoshop using a Wacom tablet and various textures. However, the type for "Bold Is Beautiful" was created in 3D Studio Max. His biggest inspiration is the music he listens to and the feelings it instils in him.

Bold Is Beautiful

40

Prom Night (Bullet For My Valentine)

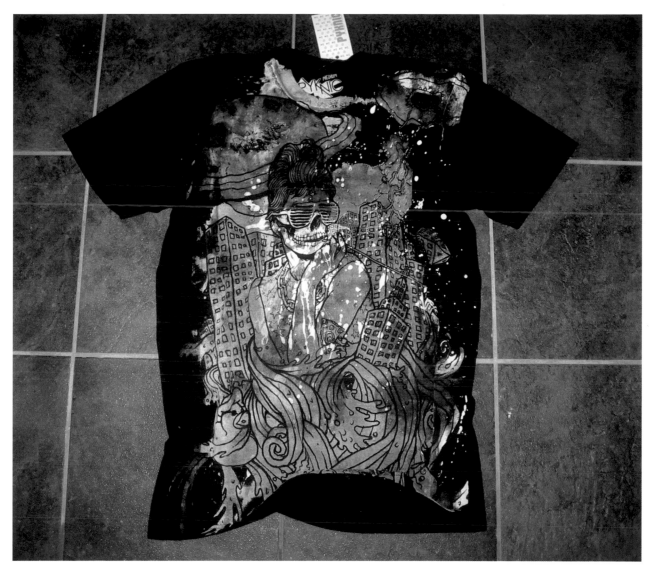

Tawdry Hepburn

VRUCHTVLEES CLOTHING

The Netherlands
www.vruchtvlees.com

Royal Blue

Bloody Red

Cocaine White

Three guys from The Hague and one bottle of whisky was all it took to come up with the freshest clothing brand the universe has ever known. Roughly translated, the word "Vruchtvlees" means "fruit-meat", also known as "pulp". The contrast between fruit and meat can be found in the designs of the first collection, handmade by the founders themselves. The Vruchtvlees brand not only stands for the clothing, it also represents their design studio, the highly appreciated Vruchtvlees parties, the mix tapes they have put out and their million euro swagger, of course.

Tandenboormachine

A long time ago, we were in the library studying physics (at our university you must study physics) and that was so boring we decided to sing a song. At that time, we thought "Can't Take My Eyes Off of You" was a Sinatra song. We started to sing and one of our friends, who can't speak English, sang "I love you baby, and if isquaronai" (which should have been "and if it's quite alright I need you baby"). We are still laughing about it, knowing our English sucks, too. Nevertheless, that was how we chose our name and we are still creating everything in that random way. We know design processes, but when we decided to do Isquaronai that was just for fun and will be this way forever, we hope!

Brazil
www.flickr.com/photos/isquaronai

ISQUARONA

Guarda-quedas

Equações De Jericó

Meu Elefante De Estimação

Anywhere Anytime

Balken

Face

Cube White

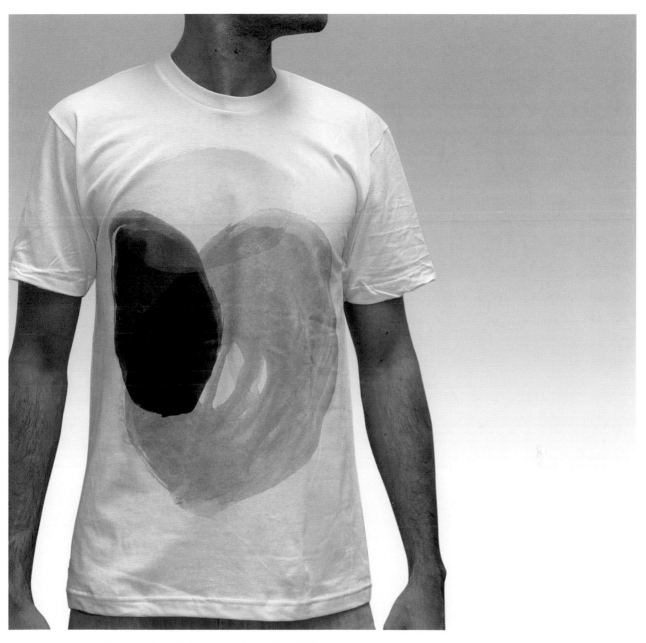

I was up to produce colourful versions of the Stormtrooper uniform - the one out of the old *Star Wars* movies. I had troubles with licences and problems defining the target group. That's why I made a simple decision to put graphics on T-shirts. Heraldic figures of love, peace and happiness! Colourful. Humorous. Playful. Typographic. Illustrative. Beautiful. Silly. Spiritual. Wise. Intelligent. Wrong. Brutal. Amazing. Heroic. Tasty. Crazy. There is a similarity between creating a T-shirt graphic and a poster graphic. I could imagine that designing a T-shirt is different from designing a spaceship. I'm not sure. I was never involved in designing a spaceship but you can believe me that I would love to.

Duppe

FALKO OHLMER

Germany
www.lesucre-clothing.com

51

Oh Yeah

Keep Smiling

Hello Everybody

Ami Ou Ennemi

Dreieck

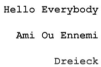

Round Midnight

Headphones

Hungry Tree

Bringing The Funk

I'm an artist from Milwaukee, Wisconsin. These shirt illustrations were created for the clothing label Heavy Rotation. The paintings are originally gouache and mixed media on paper. They were scanned in and colour separated using Photoshop.

USA
www.ricstultz.com

RIC STULTZ

Thunder City

Sheriff

The Blues

Record Player

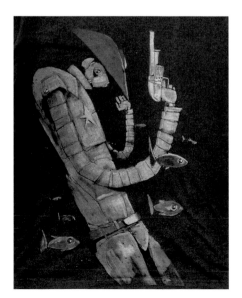

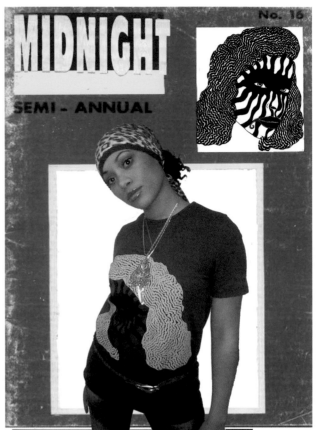

Chi Chi

Zigzag

Sir Fearnot

Brennan & Burch are a colourful and imaginative British streetwear brand designing quirky but highly wearable casual wear with bold, original graphics. Collections are always eye-catching with the Brennan & Burch signature style - a strong look mixing imaginative illustrations with fashion-forward shapes for women and men. The brand, established in 2001, designs and manufactures in the UK. New styles are continually introduced, with designs only made in limited quantities. Designer Lisa Brennan originates from London, where she beavers away designing her signature fun, quirky fashion in a make-believe world of her own. Lisa has established herself as an up-and-coming illustrator. She is self-taught, with a heavy emphasis on hand-drawn fantastical graphics. Lisa's designs have been used on clothing, belts, bags, caps, flyers, shoes and wallpaper and have graced the pages of many international magazines.

UK
www.brennan-and-burch.co.uk

BRENNAN & BURCH

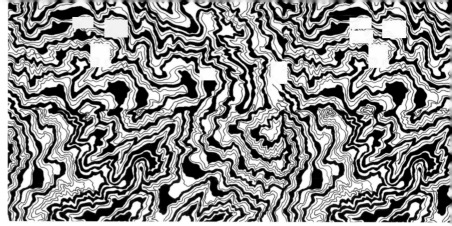

Butterfly Skull

Cat Star Tree

River Runs Deep

X-Ray Specs

following pages:
Monster Sheriff

Sacrifice

Optical

Wow!

Over And Over

Untitled

Mickey 3D

Smiles

Giletes

Listras

Degradê + Desenhos

My T-shirts are all
hand-crafted with tools
appropriate to fabric. My
inspirations are cartoons;
art, particularly pop art;
children's drawings;
animals; my daily stories;
my family and friends.
I try to transform my ideas,
feelings and thoughts into
art, often expressing myself
by taking pictures.

DOUGLAS CARLOS DA SILVA

Brazil
dcdsbitchwear.blogspot.com

Robots Attack

BLACK ROCK

International
www.blackrockcollective.com

COLLECTIVE

The Black Rock Collective (BRC) is a community of artist friends who take joy in working together and helping each other out. With the aid of each other's critiques, the individual members continue to grow as artists.

The BRC was formed after a group of very talented designers met through an online T-shirt design competition, on the internationally acclaimed Threadless.com website. A few of these pale, creative people started to seek advice outside the community's all-seeing eye, and began communicating with each other directly. As time passed, the BRC grew in number through mysterious initiation rites. Each designer's strengths convened with the group to become something even greater. Soon, there were masses of designs to be critiqued, projects to be organized and collaborations to take part in. The BRC's combined powers coalesced into a brand new community and groundbreaking ideas formed.

The Revenge

Altitude Sickness

The Black Dahlia Murder - The Mummy

Set Your Goals - Sea Life Extravaganza

Viatrophy

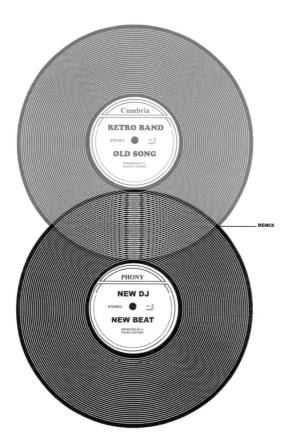

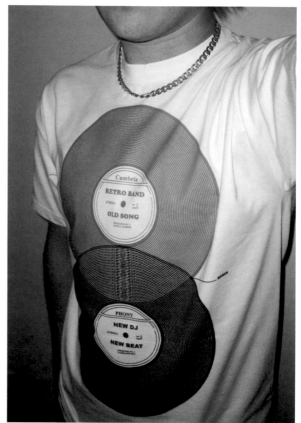

Remix

88 Ghosts

Good Blood, Bad Hands

Dashboard Confessional

Longarm

HORT

The concept was not just to design some nice shirts. We are educated so we wanted to have something with a theme. We chose Dostoevsky as the base for our designs. We built a font out of fragments from Russian architecture and these shapes became a system with which we were able to play. Our designs feature different spot colours on plain white shirts, plus an extra label. T-shirt design is just another format, and it's wearable. You can, if you want to, play around with the material and the person who is wearing it. This can be part of your concept. We appreciate the limitations of T-shirt design. Limiting yourself can be very good in a design process. We don't consider our shirts art. It's fun and a statement – if we like it, we wear it. However, in a way we are not really thinking about it.

Germany
www.hort.org.uk

Educated Fanbase Collection

Der Verstand

Chandelier T-shirt

Dostobeard

Big A Hort

Mond

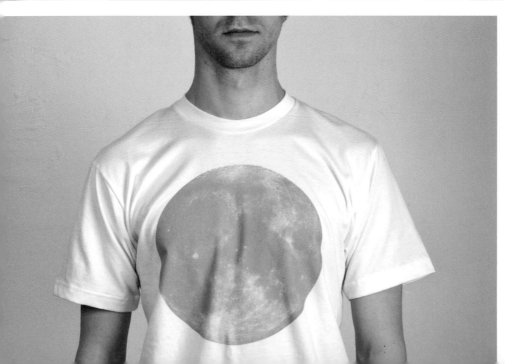

UK
www.iloveboxie.com

I LOVE BOXIE

Hey,
you and I
are going to have
a big
love affair
and it won't work
but somewhere in
the middle
my god, we tried

I NEED TO REMEMBER HOW I FOR GOT YOU

I LOVED HIM,

TELEPHONE ME

THE DOG THAT BUILT THE SKATE PARK

I'M WITH DUCK WOOD

MY DADDY WAS A REVOLU TIONARY I CAN'T GET A JOB

WE'LL NEVER HAVE & ENEV

In 1978, a T-shirt maker went missing. His last word was "Boxie". The I Love Boxie company is the story of how we got to Boxie. Our T-shirts mark the way. Each one is about a place we have been or someone we have seen. Stories, about big loves, small breakfasts and people with nice hair, can all fit on to T-shirts. Some tell a line of our customers' stories. If not, there is our customized service, T Spoke. This is where our customer calls us, tells us a story and we come up with one line that we hand-print on a T-shirt. Even if it is the greatest line we ever come up with, we will never ever resell it to another person.

GABRIEL RICIOPPO

Ser-vice is a lifestyle brand focusing on clean aesthetics and modern lines. Our approach to life is simple yet very detailed. We look for the best in everything and love what we do. Our roots are in graphic design, but we are driven by architecture, furniture, good food, friendships, surf trips, flip tricks, photography and smart design. We strive to produce items that we enjoy ourselves and our friends are proud to support. Through our view of environment and culture we look to improve the aesthetics of our world and yours. All of Ser-vice's items are produced in limited numbers, with attention to detail and quality. We stand behind environmentally sound elements and incorporate them whenever possible.

Australia
www.serviceisgood.com

Bars

Circle

Ampersand

Zebra

Tape

Grey Clouds Glad Me

Moustache

This Mess You're In

Serial Cut is a Madrid-based
studio focusing on art
direction, graphic design
and illustration and working
for clients internationally.
These T-shirt designs
were conceived to wear a
message, usually in an ironic
way. Miss Minou does the
illustrations and the Serial
Cut team chooses the type.

SERIAL
CUT

Spain
www.serialcut.com

CHAD EATON
TIMBER!

TIMBER! is an entire line of T-shirt designs based on a story about lumberjacks, their bosses (guys with top hats and cursed with excessive hair) and Bigfoot stuck in the middle. The story gets more complex with every design. I am adamant about keeping to the theme. Therefore, I alter ideas that don't really fit into the TIMBER! world until they do. Currently, I hand draw and print every shirt. There is much to consider when designing a T-shirt. I think size, placement and colour scheme are most important. The thickness of the ink, the weight of the T-shirt material, the size of the shirt; these are all things to consider in the initial stages of design. Even though I do many different types of art, I always come back to the T-shirt, because it's probably the most accessible medium out there.

USA
www.timberpreservationsociety.com

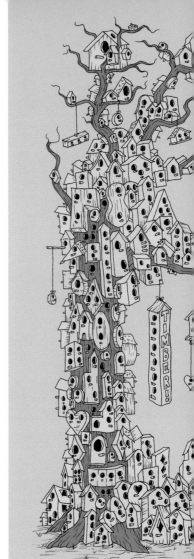

Village

Stockton

Logs

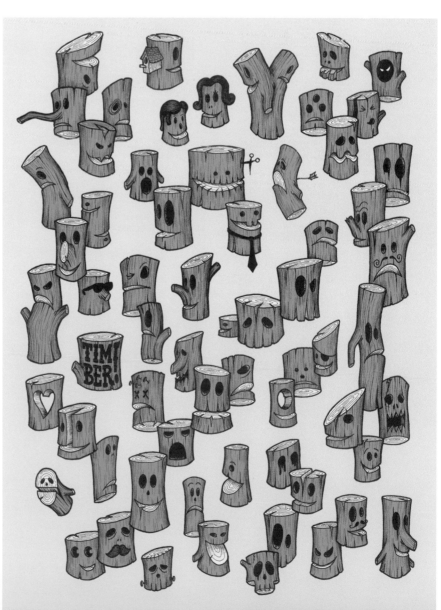

Balloon

Corporate Machine

The Tree

Giants

Movin' Out

ZOSEN INTERNATIONAL

Born in Buenos Aires in 1978, Zosen's first contact with street culture was "skating" and, after that, graffiti. Influenced by the punk/DIY movement, he was initially self-taught and later studied art at the School of La Lloja of Barcelona, becoming a Superior Technician of Plastic Arts and Design.

He not only dedicates himself to graffiti, but also has a clothing brand Animal Bandido, of which he is the designer, together with Claudia Font. They intend to create a different style within streetwear, which at present is dominated by multinational companies that blow up prices with their production in the Third World. He participates in exhibitions and special events, both nationally and internationally. His work has been exhibited in European and American galleries.

Brazil
www.animalbandido.com

Cabaret Macabra

Guerrilla Acida

Tofu League

Folklore Combat

Tourist Terrorist

I like picking imagery I find interesting and finding ways to make it work in a T-shirt design, without it being too arbitrary. My concepts are usually not terribly strong, so I try fighting with visuals instead! I challenge myself in some way; whether it's through the limitations of the shirt, the subject matter or working through conceptual ideas. I also take into consideration who would buy it. Start to finish, these are Photoshop products. It's most efficient for me to plan, sketch and redraw within the same digital canvas. I especially love working with limited colour palettes for screen-printed designs. I think a limitless palette is overrated - at least if you're going for a strong, graphic style. Sometimes the canvas of the shirt works to a disadvantage, but it's fun to brainstorm ways to work around it. With these works, I was very inspired by the iconography of secret societies, mysticism, Native American cultures, space, animals, geometry ... but this may all change in time to come.

JULIA SONMI HEGLUND

Life Prism

Daydream

USA
www.sonmisonmi.com

Fox And Hare

Secret Society

Believe It

IN BLACK WE TRUST

IBWT is a personal creative space created for enjoyment, research and development of unique products. It is a space that, from its conception, avoids mass-production systems. The actual place in which all this occurs is a small screen-printing press created by the recycling of waste materials. For each product the technique used depends on the materials available, but the shortage (or randomness) of material is overcome in the creative process.

Spain
www.inblackwetrust.com

Labyrinth Skull
front and back

Run DMC

Elvis

Run DMC & Elvis back

2face

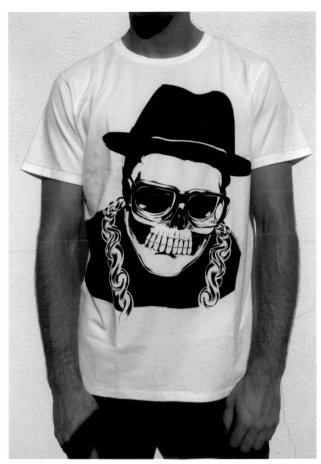

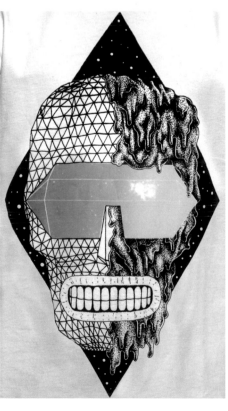

Turntable Tourne Disque Drawing

Turntable Tourne Disque Drawing
back

Ian

Ian
back

B

MWM GRAPHICS
MATT W. MOORE

USA
www.mwmgraphics.com

I try to portray an abstracted and scrambled alternative reality. I wear my own shirts almost every day! I often use vibrant colours, clean asymmetrical geometry and a story. I try to have a narrative for each design, so it tells a visual story. The featured designs involve mostly vector graphics in Illustrator, but some are hand-drawn and hand-painted. Shirts are fun because they are in three dimensions and exist in the real world. I thrive when limitations are present. Some of my favourite recent work was achieved with only three or four colours. It makes me happy to see people wearing my designs. Life, nature, maths, family and love inspire me. I like the freedom to play and explore. Most of the time tees are just meant to look great, and there are fewer hoops to jump through than on other design projects.

Art Is Not Mute

Angular Art Degrees

MWM X AUDIO AESTHETICS. Art Is Not Mute.

Life Of A Tree

Blood Is The New Black

TT Mountain

Critique

Ludwig Van The Man

Spaceknuckle

Dead Artist Society

Tank Theory

Official

Ludwig

Mandala

MWM x Blood Is The New Black

121

C-O-L-T-E-S-S-E

Nike SB I

Nike SB II

Blood Is The New Black II

Graphic Endeavors

Durkl

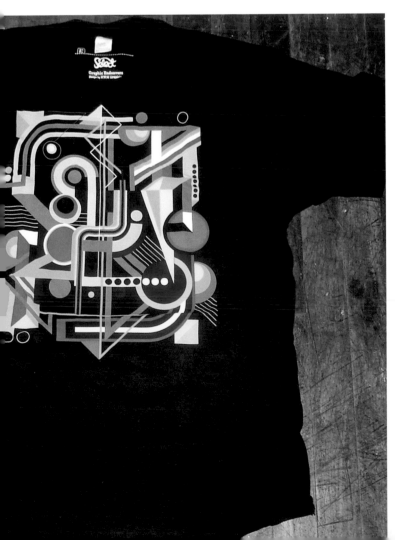

Technicolor Dreamcat

Avenger African Safari

Rosebud

Avery Island

124

Los Angeles-based illustrator Hannah Stouffer finds a great deal of comfort in imagery – it's an admiration that is often overwhelming. With an infatuation for icons and images that reflect and categorize historical eras, genres and subcultures, her work is an opulent, elegant and beautifully intricate mixture of illustration and design. Her densely packed compositions consciously recall classical elements from our past and combine them with our modern attractions, creating cohesive yet opposing arrays of imagery and embellishment. She focuses on the contrasts between periods in time, subcultures and social trends – and merges them together with a high regard for traditional decoration.

HANNAH STOUFFER
GRAND ARRAY

USA
www.grandarray.com

Until It Becomes Her
Brenda Revisited
Night Whispers To Me
In These Arms I Keep
Le Beau

Elegance

Animal Kingdom

Dust To Dust

Medusa Jungle Tour

Roots

HAPPY LOVERS TOWN

It's a really simple concept ... enjoy and spread love. Trademarks of my designs are less colour, less form, more "amore". The origin of this design comes from the idea "simply tee, simply work. I think cotton and samba". I'm in love with limitation. I based each work on simple limitation. And like all designers, I live by the idea "less is more". It's funny that people wear my art. Children's books by writers like Emberley or Eric Carl inspire me. I like designing shirts because it's a joke; I'm in love with humour. Currently, every day I draw tees and tees and more tees. It's a strange moment.

Italy
www.happyloverstown.eu

People Love Strawberries

A Smile For Timbuctu

The Diver

Icecream

Venetian Blind

Shoulder Bag

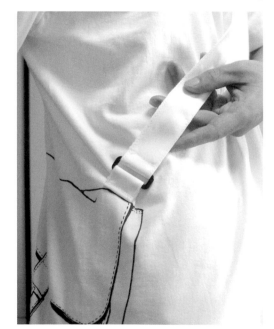

NOTO FUSAI

Shikisai is a T-shirt brand launched by designer duo Noto Fusai that explores the possibilities of T-shirt design using only white T-shirts and black prints. They use familiar motifs such as venetian blinds, plugs and sneakers, and give pleasant surprises to those who wear them or see them worn. The last name of the talented husband and wife team is "Noto". "Fu" means husband, and "sai" means wife. All together, Noto Fusai stands for "Mr. and Mrs. Noto".

Japan
www.shi-ki-sa-i.com

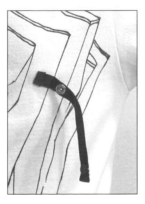

Canvas Shoes

T-shirt

Umbrella

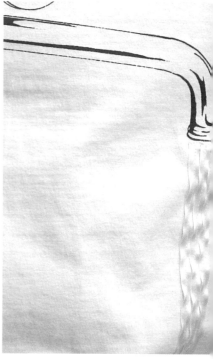

Bath Plug

Faucet

Tricycle

Reversi

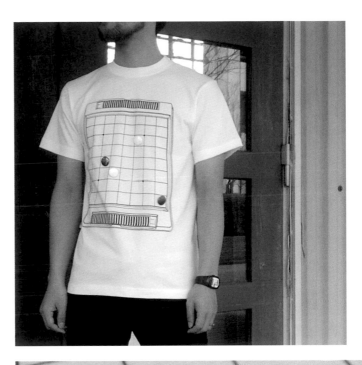

Got To Have Balls

Periodic Table

Face

Wise Monkeys

Apple Skool

Jan Kallwejt, born in 1981, is a graphic designer and illustrator from Warsaw, Poland. "I am satisfied with many of the designs I do; I feel like I am creating them for other people. There are some T-shirts I design specifically for me to wear. You have to remember it is not just a design; people will wear it, there is a fashion factor to it. I like to see my designs printed on fabric and I like that they become part of people's wardrobes; they wear them so they also become part of their lives. Usually, I am limited in the number of colours I can use, which is fine with me, as I prefer using only two or three colours. Exploration of themes inspires me. I have my own T-shirt brand; I design at least two or three T-shirts per month. I also occasionally collaborate with several other clothing labels."

Poland
www.kallwejt.com

JAN KALLWEJT

MATTHEW WAHL

I designed all these shirts for my job as the art director of a Christian ministry. I am obsessed with type, and I enjoy being able to incorporate my own typefaces in my designs (such as the "... And I Ate Them", "New Attitude" and "Read™" shirts), but I think typography functions best when it reinforces the underlying concept. For example, the profits from the "Uganda" shirts went towards building wells in Uganda, hence the U functions as a stylized well; the empty letters in the "Sans '05" tee reflect the cancellation of an annual conference that was then brought back by popular demand. I think T-shirt designs can be more enigmatic because the wearer can explain the design to anyone who asks, starting a dialogue. My main goal is to create designs that are smart, engaging and well-crafted, and if they end up looking cool, that's just a bonus.

USA
www.flickr.com/photos/secondscout

Sans '05

If Then Na

Alphabet Tee

Na Promo Shirt

Read™

New Attitude

... And I Ate Them

Together

Meat Me Inside

Disco Moon

Chop Suey Attack

Bounty

We have worked on several
themes for our shirts,
from embryology to past
predictions of the future.
However, we always lose the
grip in every project. We
think about some situation
and the designs go deeper
than we expect. We guess it
is because there are four
creative minds taking control
of each design. Of course, we
have a common understanding
in taking positive sensations
in every piece we create; on
the other hand, maybe not.

MOPA

Brazil
www.estudiomopa.com

I try to make as many tees as I can, because it's a job and at the same time a way to express myself. The idea is to show something strong, extreme and firm that says something about the attitude of tee owners in comparison with everyday human life. My work is self-confident but also self-ironic. Each time I draw the feeling is unique and beautiful.

Italy
www.thomasray.net

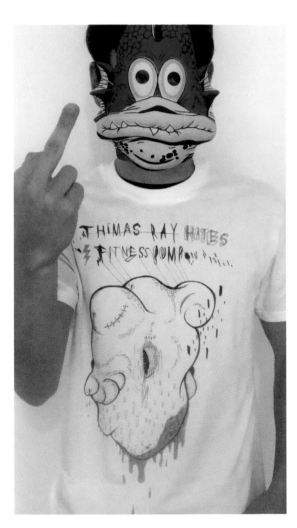

Thomas Ray Hates Fitness Pump I

Thomas Ray Hates Fitness Pump II

Live Forever

Mr Nebula

Fuck

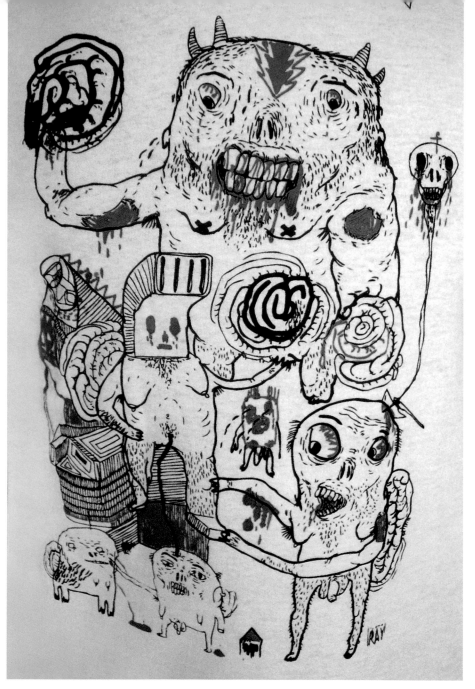

Quarter

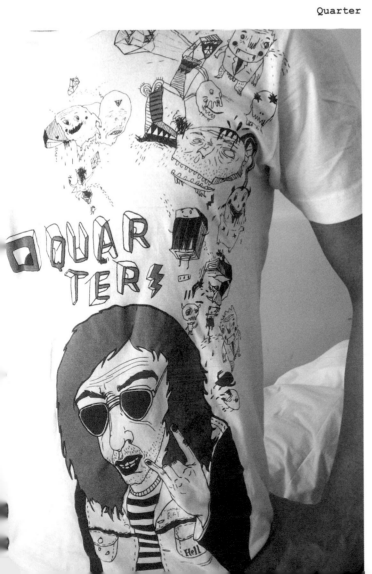

2SICK
BASTARDS

UK
www.2sickbastards.com

2SICKBASTARDS
- Purveyors Of Quality Shit -
We are not you, we're not
just doin' it, we're not
lovin' it and we are not the
real thing. There's two of
us, we're too sick and we're
bastards - put simply, we
are 2SICKBASTARDS. We create
artwork, design T-shirts
and generally make money
out of other people's misery.
Top-selling designs included
Dubya and Saddam kissing,
Britney and Christina
enjoying double-ended fun
and Kate Moss suffering the
side effects of enjoying
too much "cola". More recent
designs feature an identikit
Jacko, Trekkie loon Tom
Cruise and old favourites
Mr. T and the Hulkster.

following pages:

Double Trouble

Britney Tears

Little Bastard

Cruisology Kills

Misfit

Enjoy Kate

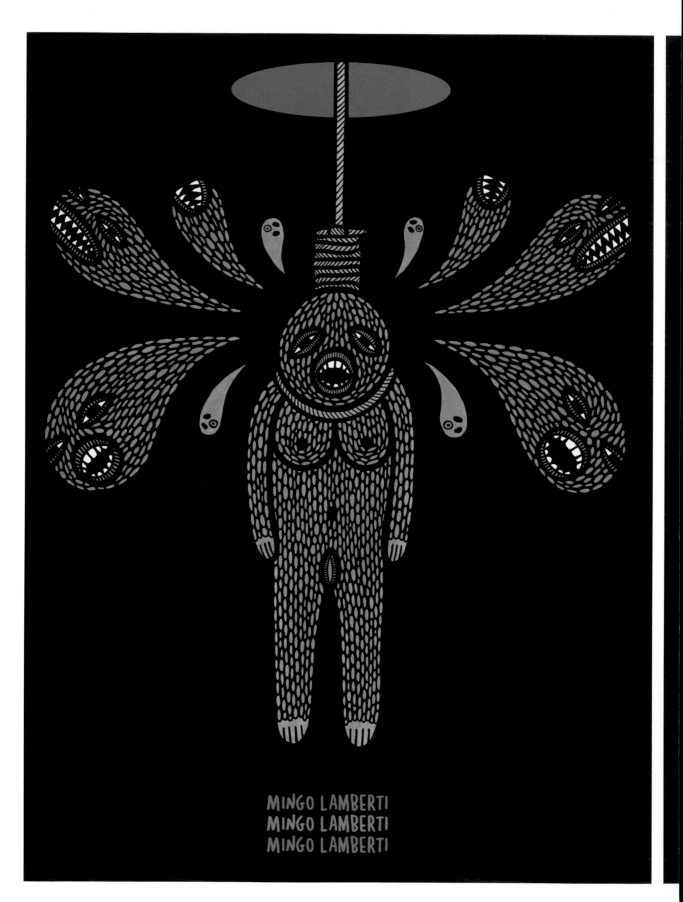

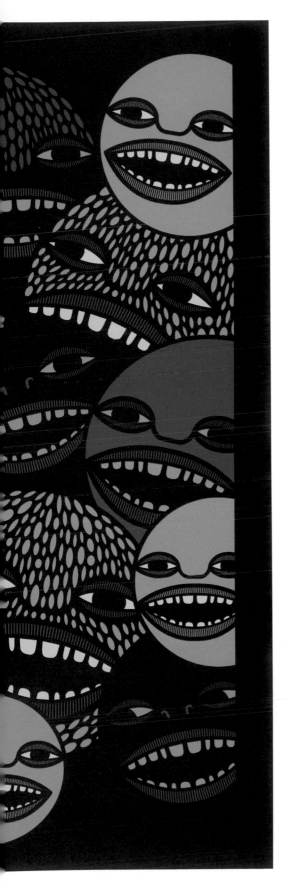

BEASTMAN

Australia
www.beastman.com.au

The theme for the "Mingo Lamberti" shirt was "Death", so I did a guy hanging himself. I used acrylic, ink on paper, scanning and Photoshop. "Folklore" was designed with a vector image created in Illustrator. Unique to my designs are the characters. The limitations of T-shirt designing differ from other designs and are therefore a challenge. When designing a shirt, the colour of the shirt, the colours in the print (depending on the printing budget) and placement of the print on the shirt are all-important. You also always need to consider how it will look when someone is wearing it. Shirts are like moving art galleries. Friends, other artists I work with, music, nature, heraldry, symmetry, skateboarding and stupid people inspire me. I design shirts occasionally, when a brand/label approaches me to do a design. I feel weird wearing my own shirts; I usually give them to friends.

Mingo Lamberti

Folklore

Neue Haas Grotesk – Switzerland 1957
Max Miedinger / Eduard Hoffmann

Weight Series

Weight Series is a series of shirts where the weight of the typeface determines the size of the garment or (more typically) the weight of the user. We had this idea in our heads for several years but it was not until the 50th anniversary of Helvetica in 2007 that we decided to put these items into production.

FTBLL T-SHRTS were designed to celebrate the 2006 World Cup. Created for people who enjoy football and want to support their team, they offered an alternative to the mainstream football kits or the usual run-of-the-mill merchandise on offer to football fans during the festivities of the World Cup.

UK
www.blanka.co.uk

MARK BLAMIRE
BLANKA

Untitled

Fluffy's

The concepts behind our designs depend on the client and their needs as we produce many designs for clients and not just for ourselves. We are not very good at making back-ups or reproduction of our work. Usually once finished we pass on to something else and forget about it. This is the first time we have made a small effort, have had them worn and taken photos on a white background. However, we are working on a monograph for which we have asked a photographer to take pictures of our designs. There are several differences: the fact that you are working on volume (on the body) on textile; the fact that the design will evolve (being worn and washed); and maybe the visibility. We like the possibility with the silk screen of having a limited production. The T-shirt design is maybe the work in which we have fewest limits.

Switzerland
www.happypets.ch

HAPPYPETS

Booby Barn

No Bread Just Meat

Never Watch The Sky

Blind Stomach

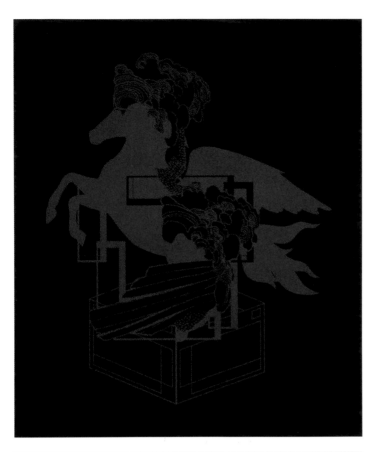

© happypidgn

JAN AVENDANO

Canada
jarnmang.blogspot.com

Jan Avendano is a graphic designer and illustrator currently working out of Toronto. She enjoys doodling, drawing lines and monsters, good food and a hot cup of coffee. The concept of her designs changes with each work. With her monster-based designs she tries to place them in settings that would be familiar to the viewer, but with a twist. There's a big emphasis on line work so most end up having hair or fur on them. The designs usually start out as doodles or notes in her notebook and then she'll take those ideas and start drawing them in Illustrator with her tablet. When designing a shirt, the shape of the tee plays an important part in the layout of her design. She considers how something will look at different angles and how sizing and placement of it will change the impact the design will have.

And How Are You Feeling Today?

Freeloader On The Yak Express

Pollute

DAS MONK

When I am designing, I will have about three months' worth of ideas banked up in my head. I take ideas from various images and melt them down into one simple concept. The images featured are sketches drawn in Illustrator later. These were the last tees to use computers in the design process ... everything is hand-done now. I like a range of tees that look good together but are all individually quite different.

The theme is dictated by my current mood and inspirations. The only specific thing that is a big no for me is messages and writing on tees ... not my kind of thing at all! Designing T-shirts is a personal way of seeing people enjoying your art. The greatest sign of approval is someone proudly displaying your art on his/her chest! Tattoo artists must be in heaven.

Australia
www.dasmonk.com

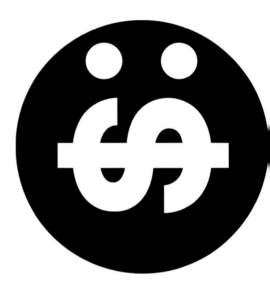

Jaws

Dollarface

Aok

HERMAN LEE FOR
FRESHFAUXX

Herman Lee is a 22-year-old guy based in Hong Kong. He moved back there after 14 years in Toronto, Canada. He got his big break in T-shirt design when his "Mona Prankster" was printed by Threadless. After that, he started to do tee designs for an assortment of big and indie labels and submitting his designs to a variety of tee contests under the alias "dhectwenty". His tee design styles range from vibrant usage of colours to abstract images with a limited colour palette. He constantly experiments with a variety of styles for his designs.

Hong Kong
www.freshfauxx.com

Splatterbird

The Source

F.A.C.E.S.

TO

The Harder I Work

The Season Has Landed

Migratory Pattern

following pages:
The Poetry Of Demise

Synchronizing Phase

173

Don't Die

Adult Swim

The idea behind the "Tim And Eric" design was to represent the crude weirdness of the Tim and Eric Awesome Show, Great Job Tour 2007. I wanted to feature both Tim and Eric prominently, but not alone. The heart was a good addition. Either you love the show or you hate it. It is a great show to design for because anything goes, the stranger the better, no crisp clean photos or type; you have to forget what you know about design. The materials I used were a computer, a photocopier and a marker. When designing shirts they need to be wearable (would YOU actually wear it?) and keep your audience in mind (who will want to wear it?). You are selling a product and when you see people out wearing it, it gives you a feeling of accomplishment.

HUNTED DOWN

USA
www.hunteddown.com

Ignignokt

Kill

Tim And Eric

Out To Sea

Victorian Typewriters

Horse Run

We gather inspiration from a variety of sources and our themes and shirt designs change seasonally. On one occasion we were flipping through old *Playboys* and got totally inspired and created a series of designs around photos we found. We really like juxtaposing old imagery with a more modern aesthetic. The great thing about having your own brand is that, creatively, you can do whatever you want. You are your own client. There really is no one to answer to. We work in advertising and PR, so working on something sans clients is not only liberating, it also keeps us sane. We didn't set out to create a brand for the masses. We created it more for ourselves and our friends. The brand was started while we were going to college in a small surf town in California. The fashion there was and still is dominated by big name surf apparel brands. We wanted an alternative that was devoid of logos and generic artwork. It was our goal to design a brand that you couldn't find at every mall throughout the country, and what we discovered was that we weren't the only ones who were looking for more original tees.

USA
www.popjunkiedesign.com

POPJUNKIE DESIGN

Disco Roosters

Lighthouse

Model T

Space Unicorn

Lens Love

Gramophone Girl

Gun Collection

Superpredators

Give Us A Kiss

Strange Invaders

I Like To Say Things And Eat Stuff

SEIBEI is my world full of weird monsters, useless mutants and slightly off logic. Most of my "monster" pictures are actually a caricature of some element of the human condition (monsters being more fun to draw than normal people), or just something I find funny. By putting my designs out there, I want to make the world a better place for all the weirdos, dorks and whoever else. I'd like to think that I have a very personal aesthetic that I cater to, rather than working towards something someone else likes. T-shirts are different from other media because you've got to keep in mind that someone is going to want to wear this all day. They may love your style, your concept, your wit, etc., but some people just don't want to have some picture of a goofy mutant on their chest all day. Fortunately for me, some people do.

SEIBEI

USA
www.seibei.com

Sandwich Dinosaur

Ice Wizard

Thriller Was A Documentary

Vampire Career Fair

Junior Birdman

Give Us A Kiss

Oh Crap, Run Away

The Amulet

185

THE-AFFAIR

Not so long ago, a strange thing happened amidst the rubble of broken dreams and the boozers of East London. Pilgrims to this savage land decided to pool their industry experience, raw talent and shamelessly egotistical aspirations. After much beard stroking and arguing, the-affair was born. Slightly more intelligent than your average brand, the-affair makes graphic tees influenced by subjects that delve a little deeper than your standard pop references. Too highbrow? Actually, we just have a little more faith in our customers. All our shirts are printed on beautifully soft American Apparel shirts because we believe they are the best cut around. We also believe in the value of scarcity, so every shirt we produce is limited to an edition of 200. the-affair. Everyone deserves a bit on the side.

UK
www.the-affair.com

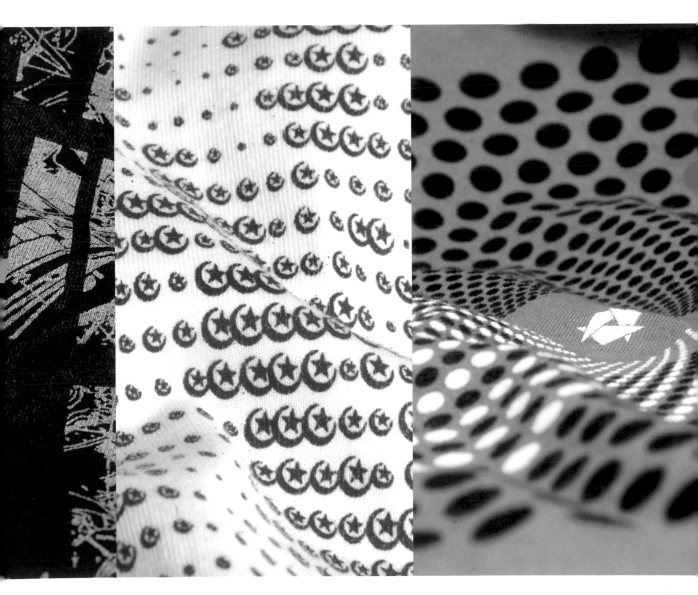

FELIPE GUGA

I am a graphic designer and illustrator based in Rio de Janeiro, Brazil. In general, I work with brands, public agencies, magazines, musical artists and editorials, but I have a special love for designing T-shirts and clothes. I like this kind of medium because I see my work on television, at the cinema, in shows and other vehicles indoor and outdoor. Besides that, it is also a medium where I have freedom to create, to show my ideas, to express my feelings and my opinions. Seeing people using my clothes, thinking similar to these ideas, is very rewarding. Through my designs, I try to show and pass on light, happy things and positive messages. I try to make people viewing them think about our human condition and motivate them to improve it.

Brazil
www.felipeguga.com

Polaroid Android

Global Warming

Fast Food

This Is Not A Sketchbook

I'm So Fashion

I Wish I Didn't Tell So Many Lies

GRANDPEOPLE

Whenever we are asked to design a T-shirt as part of a visual profile, we usually try to define it as an individual product. That means not just slapping a logo on the front, but treating the T-shirt as a completely separate entity. Our aim is to make people want to wear it and not feel like a walking ad. There are no common tendencies in our T-shirt designs, but we do make a link to the long tradition of rock and roll band T-shirts. I personally prefer a clean, plain white T-shirt, as a nostalgic reference to the time of innocence when the tee was considered an undergarment, and flashing it in public became a strong sign of rebellion. Apart from the fact that I would not call our T-shirts "art", it is funny when you see a total stranger wearing one of your designs.

Norway
www.grandpeople.org

Ekko 2007

AARON HOGG

New Zealand
www.moadesign.net

Ministry of Aesthetics is the studio of Vancouver-based New Zealand-born designer/illustrator Aaron Hogg. His interest in design began during his 12 years of recording and performing in bands. After stints as a motionographer, art director and graphic designer for the street/fashion industry, he launched Ministry of Aesthetics in the spring of 2005. The company now boasts a wide range of clients from New Zealand and abroad, including Adidas, Flow Snowboards, Kona Bikes Co., Westbeach Snowboarding Apparel, Adio Footwear, Omatic Snowboards, The Allyance Clothing, RJ Reynolds, DC Comics and Chalkydigits NZ Clothing.

Mr Choppy
Sugar And Spice
US Of A

following pages:
Pulp

Death

Killovision

Westbeach I

Westbeach II

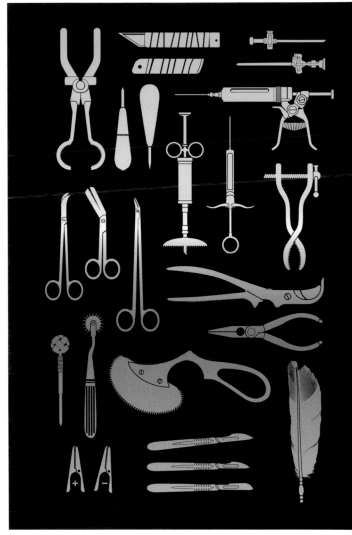

Ways Of Making You Talk

Electric Kool Aid

Kona I

Kona II

Keep It Simple Stupid

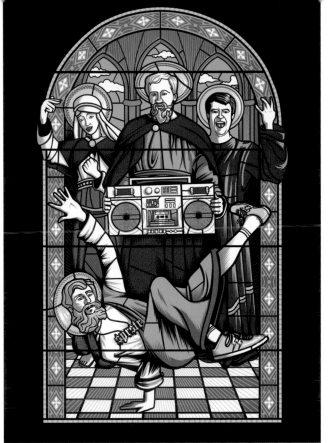

SCORE 777 OMNIPOTENCE MAX

SMITE   PLAGUE   F&B   MIRACLE   =40

SPRSTR

Playing God

Brain Dead   Mummified

Cartoons have always influenced my work, and lately graffiti artists have inspired me. *Street Sketchbook* and *The Art of Kung Fu Panda* are filled with inspiration and cool sketches. Specific to my T-shirts is a comical touch, yet still getting the main idea across. I use Illustrator and then transfer to Photoshop for textures, half-tones, etc. "Slave to Sin" utilized watercolour and line work done by hand. Some of the other pieces were hand-drawn as well. T-shirt

designing involves parameters. However, these limitations have pros and cons, as any medium does. I am venturing into print work, which allows more freedom with colours. Occasionally, I wear Rockett and Pyknic goodies sent to me, but I mainly wear plain American Apparel tees. Seeing my work purchased or worn gives me a great sense of accomplishment. I aspire to branch out into media like skate decks, posters and vinyl toys with Kidrobot, for example.

Cracked Out Cloud   Heart Of The Sun

OCKMONKEE
CHRIS SANDLIN

USA
www.sockmonkee.com

Slave To Sin

Collage

Retro

LOCOGRAFIX

Copa's collection consists of different lines with retro shirts and jackets, football-inspired printed T-shirts and sweaters, functional football apparel and footballs. My goal is to make a design that can be appreciated by all people, not only those who like football. Its design should be neutral enough so that it is attractive to anyone and just happens to have football as a theme. I like T-shirt designs with a strong image/message. All my designs have been silk-screen printed in one or more colours. Afterwards the cotton shirts have been treated and pre-washed to give them a softer touch. Designing a T-shirt is a rather small project. Therefore, you have to make decisions quite fast, which often benefits the end result. You have to be aware of the technical limitations of silk-screen printing on cotton. A good T-shirt, besides its design, is also determined by the way it has been pre-pressed.

The Netherlands
www.locografix.com

Lovallover

I Love LX

Twisted

No Pain

Vasava is a communication studio started in Barcelona in 1997. We are a team of ten young people from various fields and disciplines. We take on very diverse projects. We have a new way of dealing with the creative process based on experiment and commitment. The search for new communication values, trends and fresh ideas is what inspires us. We use a single criterion and objective to take off in different directions, working the same idea in all its possibilities and formats, capturing the most excitement we can and generating inputs. The important thing is to fix a new philosophy and a new attitude in the way our work is understood. The economical goals have been fixed as a way to improve our structure but not as our main driver. These T-shirts were designed for the Vicelona FW08 collection.

VASAVA

Spain

www.vasava.es

WRONG WROKS

Tony, born in Asia, works and lives in Vancouver, Canada. He graduated from the Emily Carr Institute of Art & Design in 2004 and started WRONGWROKS in autumn 2005. Taking contemporary cultural iconography and remixing it to his own pleasure, he has developed his own take on what our contemporary society looks like. From classic cartoon characters to famous brand names, they cannot escape The Wrong Game!

Canada
www.wrongwroks.com

Jacob

Paris

Buka Toy

American Idol

Doradimon

Dora in Pink Camo W/ Kicks

Univresity of Flaws

Spectrum

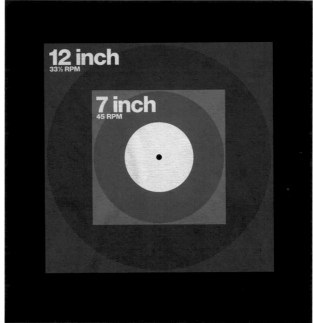

Long Live Vinyl

The movie synopsis T-shirts were based on, well, movie synopses. I was watching *Every Which Way But Loose* one night and the description of it on TV was just so ridiculous. I thought it was interesting how a feature-length film loses its impact and meaning when confined to a stripped-down single sentence. Typically, I try to use typography in some interesting way. The featured designs were silk-screened. On a T-shirt you can say "Have a Nice Day" or "Assassinate Bush". You can say that on a poster or a website as well but I think it takes it to another level when you're actually wearing it. It's a nice challenge to design something using only one or two colours. I also like that a T-shirt is similar to poster design in the sense that it should have an immediate impact and communicate its message almost instantly.

USA
www.stereotype-design.com

MIKE JOYCE

Prints Not Dead

Goner

following pages:
Karate

The Stallion

Chainsaw

Elwood

Bears

Ridgemont

Trucker

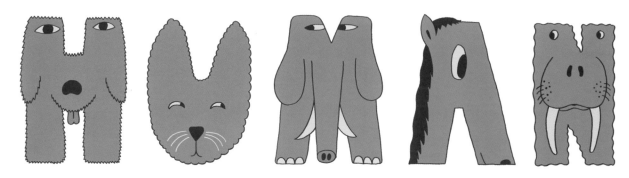

Human

Empire

Bedre!

Yokoland is a graphic design and illustration studio founded by Aslak Gurholt Rønsen and Espen Friberg sometime between their graduation from high school (2000) and their graduation from The National Academy of the Arts, Oslo (2005). Over the years, the studio's practice has taken many different directions, creating anything from awkward exhibitions and mysterious installations to conceptual graphics and humorous illustrations. This variation is apparent in the T-shirts that have been made within the last three years. There might be a lack of the conceptual work here though. Then again, not many T-shirts are conceptual anyway.

Norway
www.yokoland.com

YOKOLAND

Vampire Meets The Hound

Pirate King

Class Of 88

The Future Is History

Lovers

Dancing Shoes

Black Cat At Midnight

236

YOU WORK FOR THEM

We opened our shop YWFT in 2000, with the concept of the shop being a designer's resource for everything design. In the last year, we had a renewed desire to make shirts. One thing that I wanted to do with the shirts was to make them less "shirtish" and more in the art realm. The designs featured are either hand-drawn, digitally created, or a combination of both. We have many designers here working on different kinds of work and some of the work from different designers is passed around. Some designers living in Bangkok we (in the USA office) do not even know, or have not met. So there is a lot of room for interesting things to happen. A shirt should have a "wearable" and printable aspect to it. We can print full colour but we also like the idea of limited palettes.

USA
www.youworkforthem.com

Shapescape

Spiral

The End Up

Unibomber

Alphabet Dance

Ngoong

Two Birds Slurping On A Flower

They've Been Following Me Since I Was Little

As The Ship Approached He Offered
A Flower And Angered The Bees

A telekinetic dog stares dumbfounded at a brainwave cloud hovering, pulsing above the protruding forehead of its owner. Nearby, a one-eyed man leans into the air; his pot belly balances his bad posture. He is smiling, communicating thoughts through one vibrating eyeball. Behind him are swirled flowers, warped vegetable stalks and leafy vines spiralling upwards to a Technicolor sky. This is the cartoon world of Troy Mattison Hicks, the artist behind the quirky T-shirts known as trouble/tease. Together with Stephano Diaz, he has been creating very interesting fashion using super-cool colour gradients and candy-coloured inks to project the weird world on to cotton. Bordering on brutal, and cute, trouble/tease has both outsider art and digital dreaming to thank for the odd and beautiful pieces; fantastic and strange portraits of something completely unknown yet familiar, surreal and humorous, like snapshots from other dimensions! Welcome to the quirked-out world of trouble/tease!

TROUBLE/TEASE
TROY MATTISON HICKS

USA
www.troubletease.net

They Began To Appreciate Nature The Day The Others Came

242

Plutopian Flower

Me And My Sweet Dawg

A Many Eyed Man Stepping Over Flower

Little UFOs Aren't So Scary

243

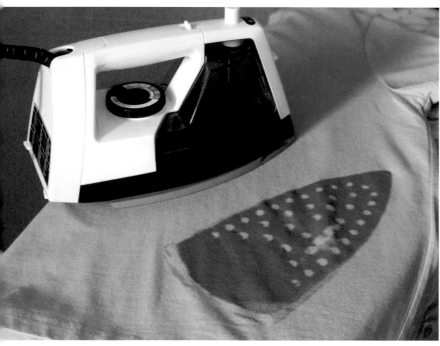

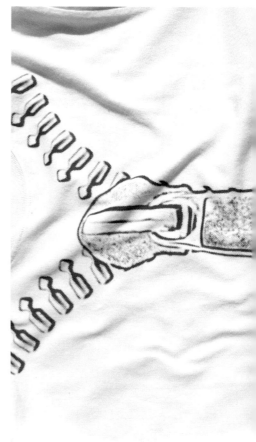

Don't Iron This Shirt

Iron Burn

RAYMOND KOO

Australia
www.takeoffclothes.com.au

Trained as a graphic designer, I worked in the design industry for six years, after which I decided to establish my own T-shirt label called Takeoff Clothing. Takeoff Clothing is a Brisbane-based T-shirt label established in 2007. The name has a double meaning – take-off as in flight and flying away, and also as in "take off your clothes!" Takeoff suggests a sense of freedom to our brand, our design philosophy and our products. Most of our ideas are very simple, yet have a sense of fun and uniqueness. We consider a T-shirt a canvas in itself. A simple idea placed on different positions of a shirt can become a unique personal statement.

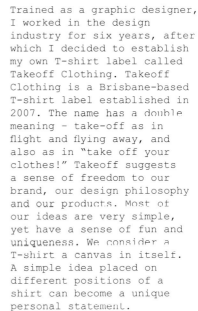

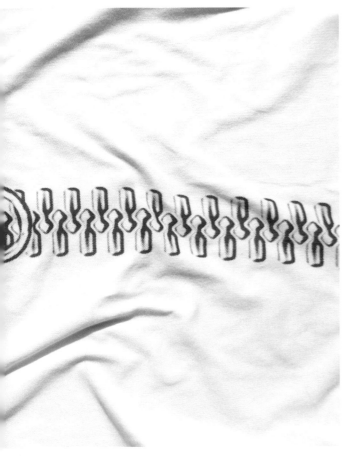

Run Over Me

Zips!

Chop

THE THERMALS

JASON MUNN
THE SMALL STAKES

USA
www.thesmallstakes.com

This series of designs was done for a project called Insound 20. Insound partnered with 20 different bands to create a line of T-shirts and I did the designs. The concepts were different depending on the band, but overall I wanted the whole series to feel like a family of designs. I typically start with rough sketches, but most of these designs were redrawn in Illustrator. These designs were also used on zip-up hooded sweatshirts so they had to be reduced to three to four inches; they needed to be easily resizable. Getting the most out of a few colours and getting images to read simply and quickly is one of my favourite parts about designing tees. For the most part inspiration comes from the client; the starting point for me is always the client. I design a fair amount of T-shirts, mostly for bands and for clothing companies.

The Thermals

Clap Your Hands Say Yeah

CONSTANTINES

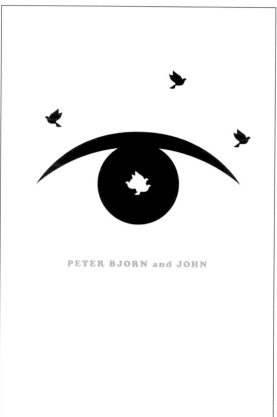

PETER BJORN and JOHN

Constantines

Peter Bjorn And John

Okkervil River

The National

Death Cab For Cutie

The Black Heart Procession

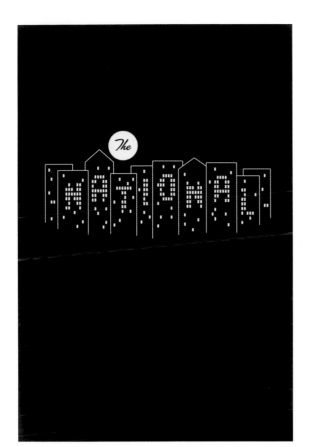

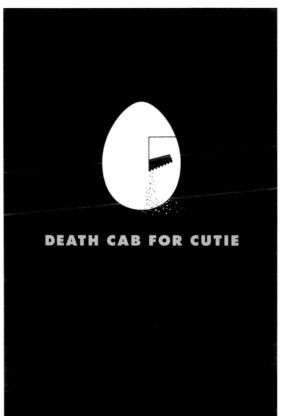

DEATH CAB FOR CUTIE

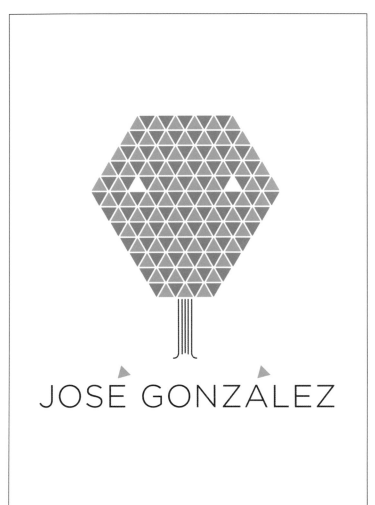

JOSÉ GONZÁLEZ

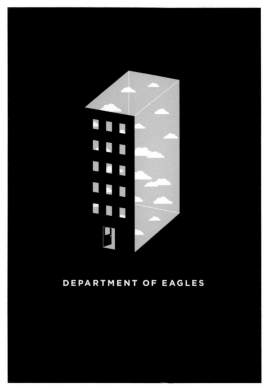

DEPARTMENT OF EAGLES

SHE & HIM

Department Of Eagles

José González

She & Him

Calexico

BUILT TO SPILL

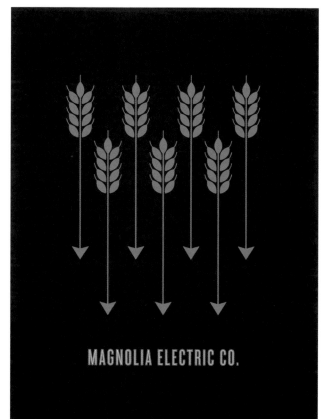

MAGNOLIA ELECTRIC CO.

GRIZZLY BEAR

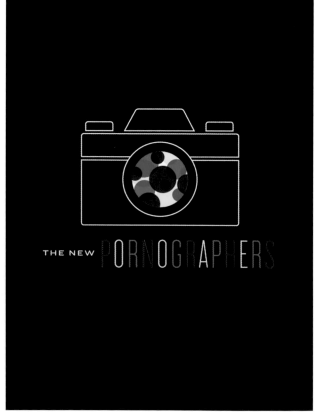

THE NEW PORNOGRAPHERS

The Hold Steady

Magnolia Electric Co.

Grizzly Bear

The New Pornographers

Spoon

Insound Logo Tee

The Decemberists

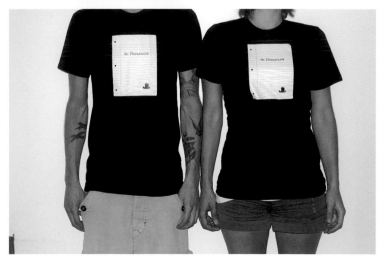

NICHOLAS DI GENOVA

USA
www.mediumphobic.com

The image is of two Siamese Chicken-Hounds. They got into a massive argument years ago when they were young pups, and they still cannot stand the sight of each other. My inspirations used to come mainly from old Japanese monster movies and various forms of street art. These days, my main inspiration is Victorian-era scientific illustration. I start with an initial black and white ink sketch, redraw it on my layout, and paint it up with animation paint, like an animation cell. Then I scan it, simplify the colours and it is then silk-screened in layers on to the tee. T-shirt designing is challenging in that the image must be simpler to allow for the screen-printing process. I like knowing that I make something people can afford to own and wear on their chests. I design T-shirts only occasionally. I have made thousands of drawings, but designed only eight or nine T-shirts.

Siamese Chicken-Hounds

Zombie Chick

Posthumous Pale Ale

BLAIR SAYER

Zombie Chick: I just wanted to design a cool zombie shirt for myself! Oh, and it had to have a hot chick on it. The client, Cleatis Preston, was completely open to it. Posthumous Pale Ale: I have always loved beer-label design and have the beer gut to prove it! I'm also a massive zombie enthusiast, so I joined both loves into a design that would be considered a convincing beer label, but also a cool T-shirt. Rabid Fire: this idea came purely from the play on words in the title. I had the idea in mind for a while, and then I found a couple of reference photos that worked together, with some artistic licence thrown in. Is Nothing Sacred: when Design By Humans had their opening competition, the US$5,000 prize was too good to ignore. I did a design with recognizable religious elements, the "sacred" idea.

New Zealand
www.blairsayer.com

Is Nothing Sacred

Rabid Fire

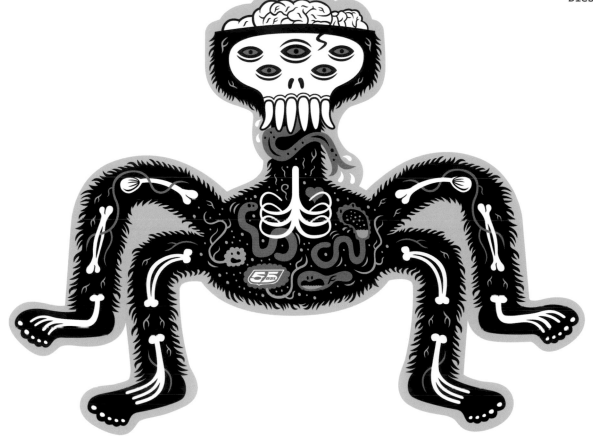

I was invited to create this shirt for 55DSL 10.55 project. The shirt will be available in summer 2009. There's not much concept to this design; it's a spider with a belly full of bugs. I designed the T-shirt on my Mac using Illustrator. You have to take colour limitations into your designs, as it's a more complex printing process and hard to get small details.

I find every new design a new challenge. I'd love to walk down the street and see someone wearing my T-shirt. I might follow them and start stalking them. Insect-eating spiders inspired me. I've made a few T-shirt designs for different companies. It's not something I do often, but if the opportunity comes up, its fun to make T-shirts.

UK
www.sergeseidlitz.com

SERGE SEIDLITZ

Misty Manoeuvres   Lifetime Laser

Trefoil Flow   Nike Perspective Type

Sweden
www.petersunna.com

PETER SUNNA

The majority of the T-shirt designs I've done have been for specific brands and the ideas were based on briefs with specific themes and often solved with some form of typographic illustration. Others are more random and simply shapes and colours I liked. I can't really say I have a specific style or something that is common for all of them. I think it depends on who the client is.

If anything, I would say I like working with typography. I like that designing a T-shirt is a small and confined project. It's an opportunity to do something different from my daytime "professional" projects. For me, T-shirts almost always are a quick turnaround job that can be more about self-indulgent graphics and illustration and less about designing by the "rules".

Lifetime Scribble

PIETARI POSTI

These designs are my personal work; they were not designed originally for T-shirts. The concepts are open; I leave them to the viewer to decide. Specific to my T-shirt designs are lots of colour, fun and flowing line work. Designing a shirt is not much different; you just have to think that the T-shirt is something personal for the user, so I always do something that I would wear myself. With modern technology and if you have money, you don't really have to think too much. Of course, there are some restrictions. For example, you can't print lines that are too thin, but I don't tend to feel limited in any way when designing a T-shirt. I dig the fact that someone wears my art! I think it's even better than some painting in somebody's living room. Comics, exhibitions, movies and everything visual in the street that pleases my eye inspire me.

Finland
www.pposti.com

GIANTS! Deer T-shirt

Escape T-shirt

Soul Sister

FORM® UNIFORM®

UniForm® is a successful design-led urbanwear label producing high-quality T-shirts and accessories. UniForm® has developed a strong fan base across the world. It has achieved sustained media interest such as press features in *Dazed & Confused*, *Mix Mag*, *Time Out*, *Drapers*, *DJ*, *Sugar*, *19*, *Arena*, *The Sunday Times*, *Kerrang!*, *Grafik*, *Muzik*, *M8*, *Cosmo Girl*, *Sky*, *Boyz*, *Elle Girl*, *Metro* (and many more), and celebrity endorsement from Dermot O'Leary, Pete Tong, Zoe Ball, Iain Lee, Edith Bowen, DJ Spiller, LTJ Bukem and Sara Cox. UniForm® was born in 1997 as a division of Form®, the award-winning London graphic design studio responsible for art directing and designing many high-profile music campaigns, including Pendulum, Depeche Mode, Girls Aloud and Everything But the Girl.

UK
www.form.uk.com

Doodle Collection:

Disko Dogg   Rock Doggs

Monsters   OK

Feed Me   Tunes

OP Collection:

Pussy

Spray

OP

Phonophobe

Chromaphobe

Rule

Cloud

LOWMAN

This design was made for a reunion party! The use of FAT typefaces is common in my style. This design was created with vectors and layers in Illustrator. When people buy and wear your shirts, it means, "You are the boss". The limitations of T-shirt design make you think more about how you experience a T-shirt and in which context someone will wear it. I am very honoured that people parted with their hard-earned cash and I hope they wear it with pride. Diverse graphical styles inspire me. I like designing because you make something that is totally yours and sell it like a canvas. This was my first T-shirt design, but I am definitely going to do this more often. I love it! I mostly wear plain colour T-shirts.

The Netherlands
www.hellowman.com

Back Once Again

SICKSYSTEM

The concept usually is a play on words and letter forms. It's all about our style. We want it to be recognizable. I hope that people will learn about what we do, not only in Russia, but abroad as well. T-shirt graphics should be pithy and self-contained. I think that you can always take advantage of any limitation. For instance, a white T-shirt with one-colour print may look much cooler than a tee with an extremely complicated and colourful design. We get inspired when we think that there are still so many cool things out there that we can do. Everybody wears T-shirts! It's a wonderful opportunity to show people our art and give them a chance to have a piece of it for themselves. Actually, we started as a graffiti crew, and now we do graphic design, illustration and some other things.

Russia
www.sicksystems.ru

272

S

Anteater

Adidas Originals
Design Challenge

Rubik's Cube promo shirts

Sicksystems

Fame Is The Name Of The Game

A-SIDE STUDIO

UK
www.a-sidestudio.co.uk

Each graphic is either an idea or a visual concept in itself; sometimes the idea will come from the client, but usually we're granted a healthy amount of creative freedom. There are no rules; sometimes the concept dictates the visual and sometimes they are pure eye candy. There's no intentional specific style. The process varies but always starts with a sketch or a discussion. The computer gets a look-in at some point; sometimes it's used to create the art, sometimes we just use it to prepare an illustration for production. There are no restrictions to creating T-shirt graphics other than the physical form of the garment; it presents a great canvas for graphic expression. Commissions usually come in the form of a loose brief. On the flip-side, it can be challenging to crowbar a graphic that has been designed for a different platform into a T-shirt format.

Art Is To Enjoy

Daydream Believer

Kernofornia Soul

Fouriron Script

Fivo

Resistance Will Grow

Think Global Live Coastal

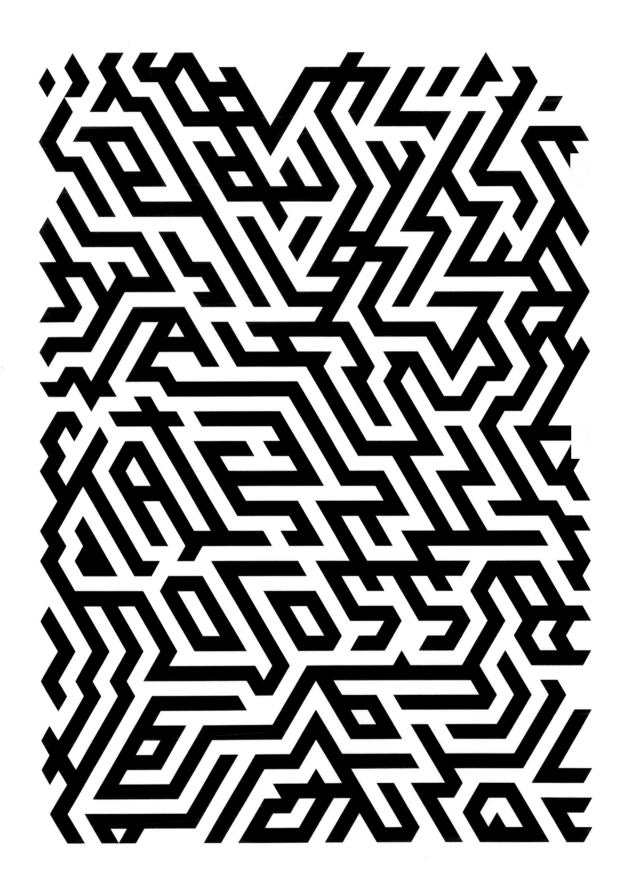

KATE MOROSS

I like to make shirts that are wearable, simple and representative of the client/band/brand for which I am designing. I wear my shirts all the time; I have no shame, and nearly 90 per cent of the shirts I wear are designed by me! My designs are bold, graphic and plentiful. Some of the designs featured are hand-drawn while others are simple digital graphics. You have to consider placement, how it is worn, what it can be worn with, why someone would want to wear it and whether it has a message or slogan on it. I love the limitations; there is still room to experiment. I love people wearing my shirts, but I have a terrible habit of walking up to people and saying shyly, "Nice shirt". Usually they have no idea who I am. Sometimes I think I come across like a jerk, but I'm only being cute.

UK
www.katemoross.com

Black & White Isometric Tee

Foil Isometric Tee

Triangle Tee

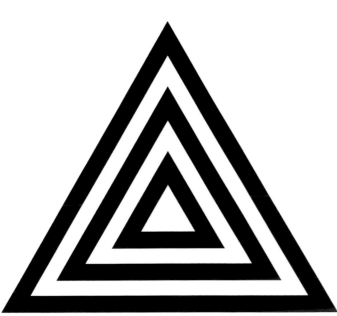

For Those In Fear Of The Lake Of Fire

The Teenagers

Punks Jump Up

Birdie Tee

Deluxe

Screaming Without Making A Sound

Eat Sleep Ride Poop

Sometimes I wear my own designs, depending on whether the shirt fits me. However, I still have them all because I like them! Designing shirts is great because it's a design with legs! What makes it interesting is that you can work with the limitations. The best part is that somewhere somebody is wearing my design; I like that. People choose it from all the other millions of shirt designs. My inspirations are mostly typography I see everywhere and cartoons. Right now I mainly do T-shirt designs.

Argentina
www.hellomaybe.com.ar

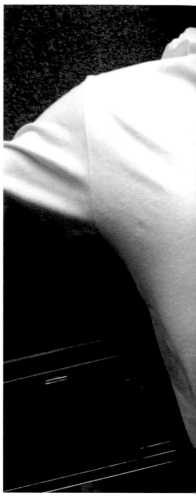

No Title

Vans+Maybe

Suba+Maybe

EDVARD SCOTT

There's a different idea behind every T-shirt. I rarely wear my own shirts. All the artwork is created in Illustrator. Different printing techniques and T-shirts (all of high quality) were used, e.g. the artwork designed for Graniph was screen printed in seven colours. Limitations force you to be more creative and I like that. Whenever I see someone wearing a piece I designed — which doesn't happen too often — it does feel a little bit strange, but in a good way. It does, however, tell me that people like to (or were forced to) wear my designs, which is rather flattering. On occasion, I design shirts.

Norway
www.edvardscott.com

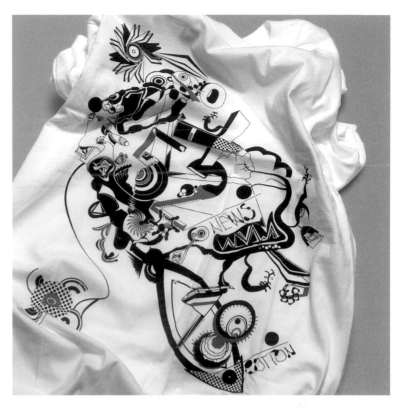

T-Post

Graniph

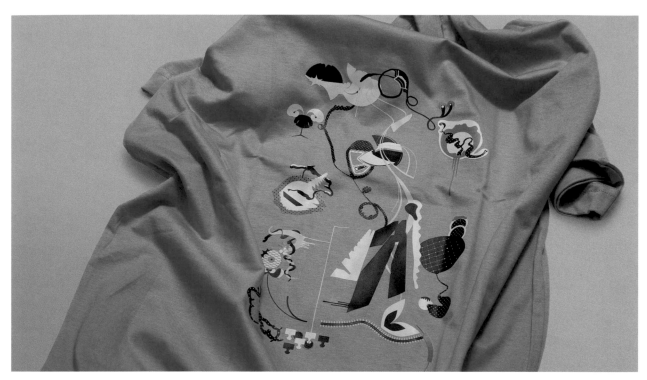

Everything Works   Computer Love

PURLIEU

The idea is that everyone living in the States (and maybe the world) is indigenous to this crazy pop culture candy-land you see on television. It's not something we crafted; we were born into it. We're all Indians in this tribe of consumerism and products, but it's also about fun! That is why we started branding our tees Native American. We are inspired by nature, indigenous cultures, Americana and Native America. All the tees are our original designs, which are first sewn from cotton jersey, then dyed and enzyme-washed, to get them super soft, and then printed. Some of our tunics are printed on the cut pieces before they're sewn together. The graphic has to conform to the size and shape of the garment, and to the shape of a person's body - a particularly important consideration for the fitted women's tunics and tees.

USA
www.purlieu.net

War Paint

Tiger Shark

Spear Heads

Candy Diamond

Aztec Lightning

Black Lightning

Fabulous Feathers

Dream Girl

Snow Leopard

Watcher

Player

Shield

Kill

Dashiki

My shirt designs are based on a common theme that we (the client and I) establish for the line as a whole. Either that or I try to draw something totally awesome. In my shirt designs, you'll generally find a common theme of hand-lettering and bizarre illustrations. My process of designing starts with a drawing, then I scan it and trace it in Illustrator to get crisp lines and finally I colour it. I like to keep my line work messy so as to keep the handmade quality, but I like the completely solid blocks of colour that the computer can provide. Designing a shirt limits me to a certain colour palette. The limitations that T-shirt designing gives me are a great challenge and I love working within boundaries. I feel like it gives my work a classic dynamic that I might not have with other forms of design.

USA
www.joncontino.com

JON CONTINO

Experience Is Everything

Brooklyn Ball

Worldwide

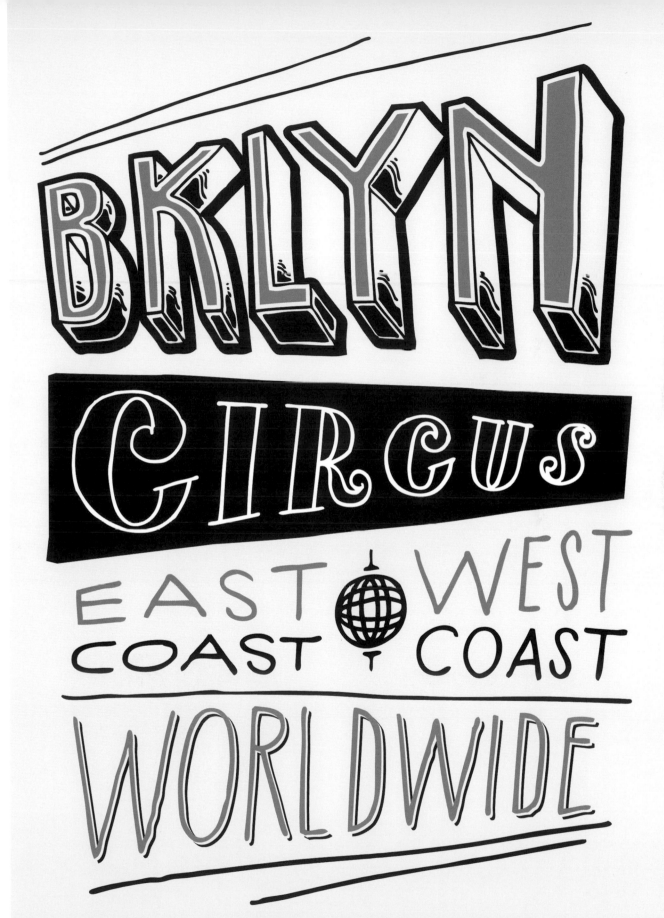

T-shirts are a great medium for our style. For some reason our often hand-drawn characters and type work really well on a tee. We usually draw everything by hand with a ballpoint. After it is scanned, we clean it up and colour it in Photoshop. Our work is inspired by many things: children's drawings, old books, television, people and many more. Furthermore, working as a duo is very inspiring and challenging.

The Netherlands
www.makimaki.nl

MAKI

Amsterdam By Night

David And Thomas Shirts

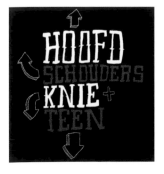

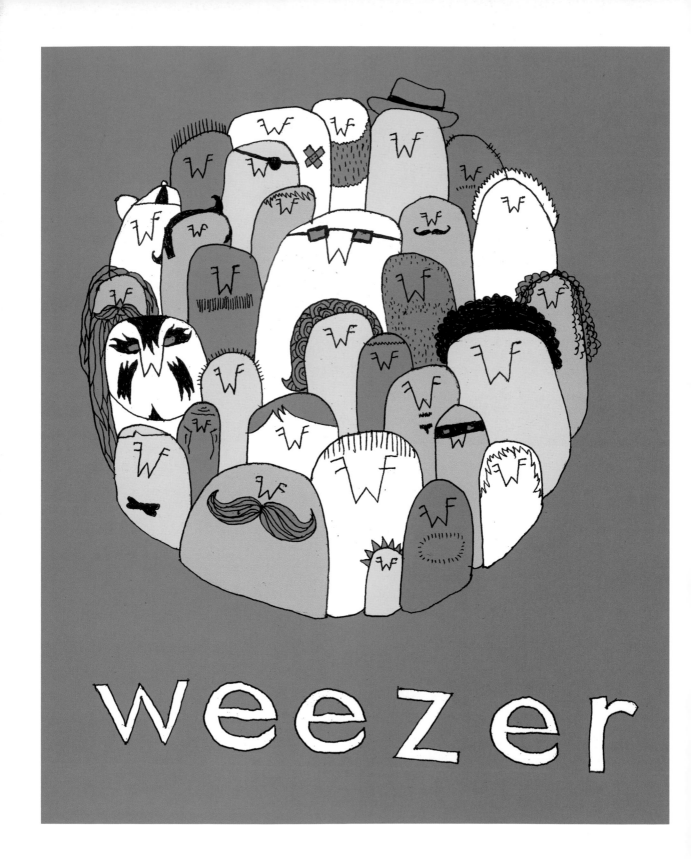

Real Men Don't Ask For Directions

Faces

Goldrush Rainbow

Evolution Of A Carrot

The Deep

Evilism

Bear Camping

Roasted Peanuts

Arab Limo

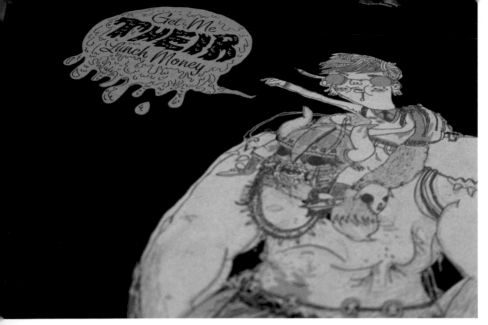

Two Man Enter, One Man Leave

I want to render things in layers, mix styles with minimal colour, to create strong 2D. In a world of lacklustre over-rendered computer graphics, I think strong two-dimensional work is important. I like to create characters. I usually start shirts with a character and expand from there; in my mind each character has a story. This cat exists, he was born in Hawaii, he has three kids and a mortgage and he's smoking a cigar and having a bad day. All the designs are made in Illustrator, with some Photoshop for colouring. With T-shirt design, I compromise less. Otherwise, I feel my nine-to-five advertising work has all the same challenges and pay-offs. Limitations make challenges fun. I enjoy problem-solving in graphic design. Dr. Seuss cartoons make me so happy. Shirts are like walking billboards; my silly drawings might be bringing milliseconds of happiness to anyone.

USA
www.agerstrand.com

JOSHUA AGERSTRAND

Zero

I Tried To Hold Your Hand

Mr. Brown

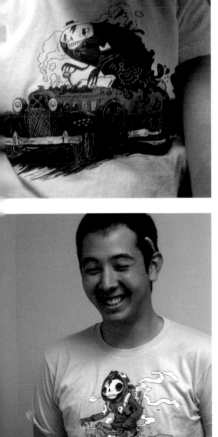

Pumpkin Eaters

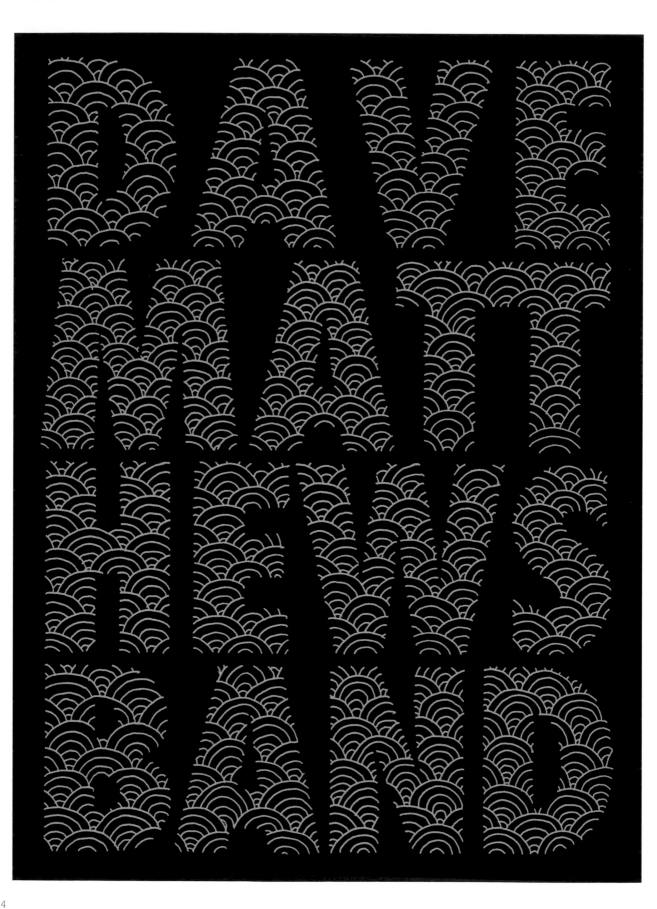

PRISCILLA WILSON

The concepts depend on whether I'm working on something for a client or if I'm submitting a design to a T-shirt contest like Threadless. If it's for a band, I usually try to listen to their music a lot before and during the design process. The music really helps inspire ideas. If I'm working on something for a contest, I just like to have fun and try out new ideas or techniques. My T-shirt designs are usually all hand-drawn with lots of line work and lots of texture.

Typically, there are lots of animals and foliage so it has more of a natural look. These designs were all drawn by hand first – I used Micron pens and marker paper – and then scanned in. From there, I coloured it in Photoshop. I do have a Photoshop Colouring Tutorial on the Threadless blogs which details the entire process.

USA
www.valorandvellum.com

Moto Jacket

Sunshine Shirt

I Love You

I Love You inside-out view

Sailing The High Trees

Sea Wolves

Sprout

Topiary

These Trees Stand Tall

MUSA COLLECTIVE

Portugal
www.musacollective.com

We don't show our names or
job positions; we show work
done. We don't show our
résumés or portfolios,
we present works. We don't
force our ideas or personal
tastes on anybody, we just
wait for your work. We are
together. On our behalf. In
the name of all. In the name
of design.

Hello World

We Want To Be Loved

Always Confused

Conspira

Pink Addiction

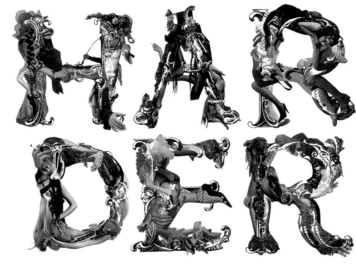

Wild At Heart

Harder

A And A

YOSHI TAJIMA

I am a Tokyo-based graphic designer and illustrator, who loves cats, curry and dance music. Based on client demand, I create as I wish. I don't wear my designs because most of them are for ladies. Specific to my T-shirt designs is the underground theme. Shirts have a different impact compared to other designs. I like the limitations because they help me be original. People wearing my art make me happy. Books, movies and daily life inspire me. T-shirts are one medium for creators. I only design shirts occasionally.

Japan
www.radiographics.jp

Daydream

CREDITS

CONTACTS
CLIENTS

If you want to find out more about a designer or a tee, you'll find the contact info here. Many of the T-shirts in this book are available through the designers' own websites, but many are available through the links to stores and through the clients below. These are in *italics*.

2SICKBASTARDS
www.2sickbastards.com
2sickbastards@pitcher.me.uk
www.mingolamberti.com
www.shotgun.tv

A-Side Studio
www.a-sidestudio.co.uk
contact@a-sidestudio.co.uk
www.uniqlo.com
www.fouriron.co.uk
www.hellogas.com

Aaron Hogg
www.moadesign.net
aaron@moadesign.net
www.threadless.com
www.cleatis-preston.com
www.goapeshirts.com
www.westbeach.com
www.konaworld.com

Beastman
www.beastman.com.au
brad@esnce.com
www.mingolamberti.com
www.folklore.com.au

Black Rock Collective
www.blackrockcollective.com
info@blackrockcollective.com
www.designbyhumans.com
www.threadless.com

Blair Sayer
www.blairsayer.com
blair@blairsayer.com
www.cleatis-preston.com
www.shirt.woot.com
www.designbyhumans.com

Blanka
www.blanka.co.uk
archive@blanka.co.uk

Brennan & Burch
www.brennan-and-burch.co.uk
shop@brennan-and-burch.co.uk

Cecilia Carlstedt
www.ceciliacarlstedt.com
mail@ceciliacarlstedt.com
www.hm.com

Coma and Cotton
www.comaandcotton.com
comaandcotton@hotmail.com
www.etsy.com

Dan Mumford
www.dan-mumford.com
dan@dan-mumford.com
thearushaaccord.bigcartel.com
www.ridetherockett.com
www.builtforsin.co.uk
www.indiemerchstore.com
myspace.com/setyourgoals
myspace.com/viatrophy

Das Monk
www.dasmonk.com
marc@dasmonk.com

Douglas Carlos da Silva
dcdsbitchwear.blogspot.com
dcds_the_strange@hotmail.com

Edvard Scott
www.edvardscott.com
info@edvardscott.com
www.t-post.se
www.graniph.com

Falko Ohlmer
www.lesucre-clothing.com
hello@lesucre-clothing.com

Felipe Guga
www.felipeguga.com
contato@felipeguga.com
www.temosdesign.com.br
www.auslander.com.br

Form® - UniForm®
www.form.uk.com
studio@form.uk.com

Freshfauxx
www.freshfauxx.com
herman@freshfauxx.com
www.luckystripesapparel.com
www.designbyhumans.com
www.bornsuburbia.com
www.threadless.com

Gabriel Ricioppo
www.serviceisgood.com
gabriel@serviceisgood.com

Grandpeople
www.grandpeople.org
post@grandpeople.org
www.ekkofest.no
myspace.com/123robot
www.tigernet.no
www.helsinkibiennale.com

Hannah Stouffer
www.grandarray.com
hannah@grandarray.com
www.thisisponyattack.com
www.poketo.com
www.bloodisthenewblack.com
www.aurevoirsimone.com
www.tanktheory.com
www.upperplayground.com
www.shalomclothing.com

Happypets
www.happypets.ch
info@happypets.ch
www.graniph.com
www.levistrauss.com

Happy Lovers Town
www.happyloverstown.eu
hello@happyloverstown.eu
www.lafraise.com

Hort
www.hort.org.uk
contact@hort.org.uk
www.azitastore.com

Hunted Down
www.hunteddown.com
hi@hunteddown.com
www.adultswim.com

I Love Boxie
www.iloveboxie.com
moxie@iloveboxie.com

In Black We Trust
www.inblackwetrust.com
ibwt@inblackwetrust.com
www.zooyork.com

Isquaronai
flickr.com/photos/isquaronai
eslsobrinho@gmail.com

Jan Avendano
jarnmang.blogspot.com
jarnmang@gmail.com
www.threadless.com
www.goapeshirts.com

Jan Kallwejt
www.kallwejt.com
jan@kallwejt.com
www.chrum.com
www.t-uesday.pl

Jason Munn
www.thesmallstakes.com
jason@thesmallstakes.com

Jeff Finley
www.gomedia.us
jeff@gomedia.us
www.designbyhumans.com
www.hottopic.com
www.pyknicwear.com

Jon Contino
www.joncontino.com
joncontino@gmail.com
www.casualtyclassics.com
www.randrtees.com
www.thebkcircus.com

Joshua Agerstrand
www.agerstrand.com
joshuapb@gmail.com
www.threadless.com
www.goapeshirts.com
www.theselectseries.com

Julia Sonmi Heglund
www.sonmisonmi.com
julia@sonmisonmi.com
www.designbyhumans.com
www.threadless.com
www.torso.com.au

Karoly Kiralyfalvi
www.extraverage.net
hello@extraverage.net

Kate Moross
www.katemoross.com
kate@katemoross.com
www.t-post.se
heartschallenger.bigcartel.com

La Camorra
www.lacamorra.com
lacamorra@lacamorra.com
myspace.com/hollywoodsinners
myspace.com/lasnurses

Locografix
www.locografix.com
jurgen@locografix.com
www.copafootball.com

Lowman
www.hellowman.com
mail@hellowman.com

MAKI
www.makimaki.nl
info@makimaki.nl
www.goapeshirts.com
www.davidandthomas.com
www.weezer.com
www.shirt.woot.com
www.poketo.com
www.threadless.com
www.theselectseries.com
www.designbyhumans.com
www.funkrush.com

Masomaso
www.masomaso.de
albert@masomaso.de

Matt Palmer
www.letsmakeart.com
matt@letsmakeart.com
www.threadless.com
www.glarkware.com
www.shirtstain.com
www.designbyhumans.com
www.torso.com.au

Matthew Wahl
www.flickr.com/photos/secondscout
secondscout@gmail.com
*New Attitude (Sovereign Grace
Ministries)*
Together for the Gospel

Maybe
www.hellomaybe.com.ar
bernardohenning@gmail.com
www.graniph.com
www.howies.co.uk
www.vansargentina.com
www.subaweb.com.ar
www.rdya.com
www.dobodob.com

Mike Joyce
www.stereotype-design.com
mike@stereotype-design.com
www.2ktshirts.com

Mopa
www.estudiomopa.com
info@estudiomopa.com
www.owlmovement.com
www.fiatfashion.com.br
www.communallove.com

Musa Collective
www.musacollective.com
info@musacollective.com

MWM Graphics
www.mwmgraphics.com
matt@mwmgraphics.com
www.tanktheory.com
www.bloodisthenewblack.com
www.ludwigvantheman.com
www.theofficialbrand.com
www.christopherbevans.com
www.coltesse.com
www.nike.com
www.theselectseries.com
www.durkl.com/shop

Nicholas di Genova
www.mediumphobic.com
medium@mediumphobic.com

Noto Fusai
www.shi-ki-sa-i.com
inquiry@shi-ki-sa-i.com
shop.pingmag.jp

Olly Moss
www.ollymoss.com
olly@ollymoss.com
www.goapeshirts.com
www.supercombo.co.uk
www.funkrush.com
www.threadless.com
www.dashboardconfessional.com

Peter Sunna
www.petersunna.com
petersunna@gmail.com
adidas
www.lifetimecollective.com
www.nike.com/nke6

Pietari Posti
www.pposti.com
pietari.posti@gmail.com
www.poketo.com
www.theselectseries.com

Pimpalicious Living
www.pimpalicious.com
info@pimpalicious.com

PopJunkie Design
www.popjunkiedesign.com
afeiger@popjunkiedesign.com

Priscilla Wilson
www.valorandvellum.com
priscilla@valorandvellum.com
www.redstarmerch.com
www.davematthewsband.com
www.designbyhumans.com
www.threadless.com
www.shirt.woot.com
www.farmaid.com

Purlieu
www.purlieu.net
skyterren@purlieu.net

Raphaël Garnier
www.raphaelgarnier.com
raphaelgarnier@voila.com
www.sixpack.fr

Raymond Koo
www.takeoffclothes.com.au
raymond@takeoffclothes.com.au

Ric Stultz
www.ricstultz.com
ricstultz@gmail.com
www.heavytees.com

SEIBEI
www.seibei.com
seibei@seibei.com

Serge Seidlitz
www.sergeseidlitz.com
mail@sergeseidlitz.com
www.55dsl.com

Serial Cut
www.serialcut.com
info@serialcut.com
www.vicelona.com

Sicksystems
www.sicksystems.ru
info@sicksystems.ru
www.anteaterclothing.com
adidas
www.respublica.ru

Sockmonkee
www.sockmonkee.com
chris@sockmonkee.com
www.ridetherockett.com
www.ephraimclothing.com
www.pts.bigcartel.com
www.pyknicwear.com
www.410bc.com

Steven Wilson
wilson2000.com
steve@wilson2000.com
www.tanktheory.com

Supermandolini
www.supermandolini.com
manos@supermandolini.com

the-affair
www.the-affair.com
service@the-affair.com

Thomas Ray
www.thomasray.net
thomasray99@gmail.com
myspace.com/fitnesspump
www.heavytees.com
www.quartershop.com

TIMBER!
www.timberpreservationsociety.com
timberps@cox.net

Trouble/Tease
www.troubletease.net
info@troubletease.net

Vasava
www.vasava.es
vasava@vasava.es

Violent Elegance
www.violent-elegance.com
hello@violent-elegance.com

Vruchtvlees Clothing
www.vruchtvlees.com
info@vruchtvlees.com

WRONGWROKS
www.wrongwroks.com
info@wrongwroks.com

Yokoland
www.yokoland.com
info@yokoland.com
www.humanempire.de
www.analoguebooks.bigcartel.com
www.notwist.com

Yoshi Tajima
www.radiographics.jp
info@radiographics.jp
ut.uniqlo.com
www.and-a.com
www.2kbygingham.com

Young Lovers Clothing
www.younglovers.com.au
lovers@younglovers.com.au

You Work For Them
www.youworkforthem.com
cina@youworkforthem.com

YUP | Paulo Arraiano
www.pauloarraiano.com
mail@pauloarraiano.com
www.ridetherockett.com
www.stationcrew.com
www.cookiefactory.dk
www.palmshirts.com
www.methodsnyc.com

Zosen – International Tofu League
www.animalbandido.com
info@animalbandido.com
www.tofulines.com

THANKS

A big hug to all contributors to this book.
Your talent made this book possible. We wish
you all the best.

We would like to thank:

Gerbrich Miedema for editing all the text,
without her on board the text would be a big
mess;

Cis, for shooting us some great studio pics at
such short notice;

Jasper, for being such a cool model;

Koen Voorend, for translating the Spanish text;

Fez, for inspiration;

Laurence King Publishing, for their enthusiasm,
collaboration, patience and for asking us to do
this project.

LAURENCE KING

Published in 2009 by
Laurence King Publishing Ltd
361-373 City Road
London EC1V 1LR
Tel: +44 20 7841 6900
Fax: +44 20 7841 6910
email: enquiries@laurenceking.com
www.laurenceking.com

Text, selection and design by MAKI
www.makimaki.nl

A catalogue record for this book is available from the
British Library.

ISBN: 978-1-85669-615-9

Printed in China